Praise

"With this book, Ms. Golinski and Dr. Becker have given both professionals and individuals valuable techniques to improve lives and protect people from the harm caused by being manipulated. It is factual, knowledgeable, and filled with practical usable tools which people can protect themselves from the destructive influence of those whose goal it is to control the lives of others."

-Maureen J. McNulty, M.S., L.M.H.C.

"How can you respond to a narcissist, manipulator, or bully? Loaded with insights, real-life examples of struggling with spontaneous responses in the most harrowing encounters, this book provides you with the communication tools, words, and demeanor to defend yourself in those challenging moments. It allows you to retain dignity and provides the calm of self-protection."

-Sandra L. Bertman, Ph.D., FT, LCSW,
Distinguished Professor Thanatology and Arts,
National Center for Death Education

"An extraordinary "how-to" book which combines psychological principles with learnable exercises and practical methods on how to avoid falling into the trap of being manipulated. This book arrives at a time when both politicians and the media have been accused of manipulating the public with biased perspectives of both the left and the right. A nation, collectively, can be as much of a victim as an individual who feels helpless. Becker and Golinski's Outwitting the Manipulator: Protecting Yourself in Real-Time Is a welcome guide, easy to read, and arrives at an opportune time for individuals and our society."

-Dr. Michael Libenson, licensed Psychologist,
Former Dean of Hebrew College, Assistant Professor
of Psychology, Boston University

"This book takes you from detection to reflection with two brilliant experts whose knowledge comes from being on the receiving end of manipulative behaviour and working with a range of perpetrators and victims over many years. It will help you to find yourself and strengthen your resolve when faced with the darker side of humanity."

**-Lynne Parker, Founder - Chief Executive
Funny Women CIC,** www.funnywomen.com

"I have personally benefitted from Dennis' expertise as a coach and can appreciate this book's expert lens on manipulation. The stories shared in this book smartly address the most common tactics and motives of manipulators and can help anyone navigate the minefields they set."

-Jon Platt, Music Industry CEO

Do you find yourself repeatedly walking away from interactions with someone in your life, feeling belittled, angry, or embarrassed? If so, you may be dealing with a 'manipulator' and not realize it. This practical how-to-guide can help you assess the situation and provides easy to implement techniques for changing it!

**-Kevin Becker, PsyD; Senior Partner
Organizational Resilience International**
www.oriconsulting.com

Outwitting the Manipulator:
Protecting Yourself in Real-Time

Robin Golinski and Dr. Dennis Becker

Spotlight PUBLISHING
Goodyear, AZ

Paperback ISBN: 978-1-953806-24-6

Library of Congress Control Number: 2021902055

Cover Design: Victoria Maxfield, http://victoriamaxfield.com
Interior Design: www.JetLaunch.com

Published by Spotlight Publishing™
https://SpotlightPublishing.pro

We invite you to submit reviews of this book.

To contact

https://www.outwitinrealtime.com
info@outwitinrealtime.com

Table of Contents

Foreword

Every one of us has been a target of manipulation. Sometimes we know it and allow it. Sometimes we know it and ignore it. Sometimes we know it and do not know what to do about it. I know this from personal experience. As an estate planning attorney and advisor to many family businesses I have witnessed countless times how manipulation occurs and its impact on a person, a family, and relationships.

In this short and powerful book, Robin and Dennis frame the issues surrounding manipulation in a manner that is clear and practical. Drawing on their years of experience as communication specialists Robin and Dennis spell out the mindset of the manipulator and the mindset of the target of the manipulation. This groundbreaking book focuses on the wisdom of Aristotle's modes of persuasion as a frame of reference. When the reader puts the effort into understanding these modes of persuasion the narrative changes and power shifts to the target. This is fundamentally important to outwitting the manipulator and the manipulation.

This book is a tremendous resource and provides valuable insights and practical tools that all of us who have ever been manipulated will find quite handy.

Patricia M. Annino, Esquire
Patricia M. Annino, Partner, Global Law Firm Rimonlaw.com

Introduction

We are both so happy to be sharing this book with you. We have observed that an enormous amount of pain and suffering is inflicted on humanity through manipulation. Manipulation occurs through communication, including withholding information and deliberately miscommunicating.

Communication is the primary tool of all manipulators. That is why we are focusing our attention on techniques in communication. Although many books deal with the psychology of narcissists, sociopaths, and psychopaths as manipulators, this book and the Outwit Phone App are different. We are focusing on 24 of the most common communication tactics the manipulator uses to control the momentum of the moment. That means body language and conversations in real-time, as the manipulation is taking place.

The primary goal of the manipulator is to control the messages and the *momentum of the moment*. They want to manage every aspect of what is happening with you. In these moments, which may be quick exchanges, a manipulator exerts great effort to influence what is happening, how it is happening, and who is being affected. Controlling the momentum of the moment is enormous for manipulators. Our goal is to give you the communication techniques that will allow YOU to control the momentum of the moment. You'll be able to react in real-time, at the exact moment of manipulation.

We understand that some manipulators may read this book and learn some new strategies. Deep consideration was taken before beginning our research and writing. We decided that creating a balance of power is more important, actually critical when taking control away from the manipulator and giving it back to you. The manipulator counts on the idea that the people they target are not savvy, capable, or bold enough to counter their tactics. They exploit normal human behavior and decency to satisfy their need for control. We want to shift the power and control to YOU.

You are going to learn how to outwit the manipulator, not only to survive but to thrive in real-time!

Ultimately the bottom line of all the advice in psychology and self-help books is to limit engagement or avoid contact altogether as you will continue to be on the short end of the stick, and the manipulator will not likely change. It can be tempting to "hope for the best" or think "things will change." None of that is likely to happen. We agree with the advice of almost all psychologists, counselors, and therapists. Get away and stay away!

The most effective strategy you can implement is having little or no contact with the manipulator. However, there are manipulators that you are related to, employed by, live near, or live with, and you will have to communicate with them until you can distance yourself. That's where this book comes in. We are using the term "target" to describe how the manipulator perceives you. We don't like the word "victim" because it reinforces the mindset the manipulator wants you to have. One of the manipulator's primary strategies is to lower your sense of self-confidence or self-worth.

So, here is one of the first lessons we want to deliver: *Don't give the manipulator control over how you feel about yourself.* Yes, it's easier said than done. Your mindset is part of how you think and, therefore, how you communicate. But you have more control over it than you know. More on that later.

As communication coaches, we have been helping clients who have been dealing with manipulation. In this book, we will share some real-life stories and examples from both the targets of manipulation and an actual manipulator.

Robin is the daughter of a manipulative mother and father. She then spent 22 years with a manipulative husband. Our combined insights as coaches, trainers, and in Robin's case, survivor, have compelled us to write this book to help you. Robin's comments and experiences are raw and revealing. She combines her personal story and professional knowledge as a communication coach in these writings. We are convinced that her authenticity and openness will help you better understand how she has come to this point and why her comments and coaching in this book are so valuable.

It is rare to find a manipulator willing to share their thinking and experience with us honestly. We found Dennis's client, Leon, was willing to share the manipulator mindset perspective. We are referring to him as a recovering manipulator rather than a former manipulator. We are fully aware that manipulators often use their expressions of remorse, openness, and seeking forgiveness as merely a different tactic for gaining control. Yet, we have decided to use some of his stories to give a rare look into the mind of a manipulator. When you meet Leon (not his real name), we will tell you why we are willing to believe him.

Here is a brief look at both sides of the manipulation story. We share Robin and Leon's perspectives to help you understand why and how we have developed the powerful and specific self-protection techniques you will learn in this book. These methods are the product of our research, the work with our clients, and our combined experience of more than 70 years as communication coaches. You can find a complete account of their stories in Chapter 10.

Robin's Story:

I've had a lifetime of being a target. It all started when I was born to young self-absorbed parents in Detroit, MI, in 1965. My Mother was 17 during her first pregnancy with me. She developed her manipulative personality based on her history. It was quite confusing as a child to have an envious, competitive, immature, exploitive, and simultaneously affectionate and charismatic mother. It was a lot to sort out when trying to grow up and make sense of the world. My Dad was self-absorbed and entitled, but my Mother was exploitative and vindictive.

My first vivid memory of the momentum of the moment or a point of psychological manipulation was at age five when I suddenly realized my parents did not know what they were doing. My father had attempted to close a broken back car door in his sedan by tying it to a headrest with a rope. There was a gap where I, my three-year-old sister, and two-year-old brother, could see the pavement speeding by as we sat in the backseat. There were no seatbelts as it was 1970. My Dad told me to keep the others away from the open door. We were driving on I-75 at 70mph. All the cars around us were waving and honking frantically while pointing at the door. I was scared of that gap, but my Dad said it was fine and not to worry about it. In the front seat, my Mother stared straight ahead and ignored us and the cars around us.

Every single passing car validated my concerns. I knew that my parents were not always right! After all, every stranger around us was distraught. That's a lot to process when you're five and trying to keep a sister and brother from falling through a crack. I share this story to demonstrate how my reality was denied at an early age - a technique you will learn about later. It actually helped me question my parents and not blindly trust what they said at face value. This epiphany was a great gift to have at such a young age.

Because I was raised by two manipulators and then married one, I feel like I have 3 PhDs in manipulative communication techniques. I'm passionate about helping others avoid being a target for manipulators. Chapter 10 is devoted to more personal stories of mine if you are interested.

Leon's story, told by Dennis:

Leon came to our office as an admitted manipulator who needed help to develop a more pleasant and productive way of getting along with people. Upon meeting with him, I immediately wondered whether his willing admission of manipulation was yet another ruse to find more sophisticated ways to manipulate his targets. It took all of my education, research, and years of practical experience to get to a place where I could accept his admissions and desire to change. Even then, I was always aware of the possibility of nefarious intent. I am sharing his story because part of it gives me a glimmer of hope. I'll share what happened to Leon and why we are including his perspective in Chapter 10.

We imagine a future where all manipulators are rendered ineffective because people with more typical empathy levels will have the tools to identify and thwart manipulative tactics. We are giving you the communication skills and techniques in this book so that you can take control of the *momentum of the moment*. As you practice and integrate these skills and techniques, you will become a very unattractive target to all manipulators. You will actually develop the ability to outwit them.

This is your training reference book. Pick it up again and again as you continue to learn, practice, and strengthen the

self-protection communication techniques. We will give you specific guidance on how to do all these things. Remember, they
are to be used in real-time, as the manipulation occurs. Learning
and practicing them makes your new response a natural reflex.
Each of these 24 self-protection techniques will be discussed
and described in detail in Chapter 6. We will refer to note-taking
repeatedly as it is essential to see exploitive patterns, develop
your skills, and deter or repel manipulators.

1

Definitions and Descriptions

AS WE BEGIN this journey to safety, self-protection, and strength, we will define and describe both Manipulation and Communication. However, before we do that, there is a body of knowledge that is the absolute foundation for persuading people. This information will be critical for you to understand. Most manipulators are already familiar with it. But, once we're done, you'll know it much better than they do. We are going to define this first because it can be found in both Manipulation and Communication. The formal name of this body of knowledge is:

Modes of Persuasion

This information comes to humankind from Aristotle (384-322 BC), the famous Greek teacher and philosopher. He introduced it in the second of three book collections. We will define the concept of persuasion as it relates to manipulation as we move through this chapter.

Aristotle believed that there are three ways anyone can be persuaded to believe anything if you choose the method with the greatest influence over the person.

The 3 Modes of Persuasion:

- Ethos (Ethics)

- Pathos (Emotion)

- Logos (Logic)

Scan the code above with your smartphone camera to watch
a short video explanation of Ethos/Pathos/Logos

As we define and explain these, think about how your manipulator may have used them. In Chapter 6, we will revisit these modes to show you how you can use them to protect yourself in real-time. That is why we go over the basics here first.

Ethos or ethics can persuade people because most will recognize you as a person of upstanding reputation, credibility, and honesty. If you have ethics, you don't need to have any other type of proof or evidence. You will not have Ethos in every situation, but only in settings where others know you to be a credible person. However, Aristotle's pure introduction of Ethos did not consider those people, especially manipulators, who have learned to fake Ethos, claiming to have ethics where none exists. The normal inclination may be to accept that a person with a fancy title must have special knowledge or qualifications. We assume they earned the job title, which gives them more Ethos. That may or may not be true, but they can claim some Ethos because they have the title. True ethics are earned and proven, typically over time and through experience.

Pathos or emotion is the next Mode of Persuasion. Pathos is the ability to persuade people because you can evoke a feeling in them. This, of course, gives the manipulator a vast selection of emotional approaches to use on you. As a quick example of how Pathos is already used on you, think about the many television commercials you have seen advertising a new car or pharmaceutical drug. Notice how many pictures you see of beautiful people smiling, having fun in the park, at a social gathering, or speeding along a deserted highway in a scenic setting... all Pathos. Because this mode is so persuasive, we will spend more time on it in Chapter 6.

Logos or logic is the third Mode of Persuasion. Logos is the use of facts, figures, statistics, and data. Logic doesn't contain any Pathos and is often seen as the opposite of emotion. Manipulators will present something as Logos when their real aim is to get a Pathos reaction from you. It is common for a manipulator to claim that they are acting logically, and it is you who is getting "over" emotional... sound familiar? This is evidence that they have identified a trigger of yours and are willing to exploit it.

Aristotle's three Modes of Persuasion will be found in both the tactic that the manipulator uses and the delivery they use in attempts to control both you and the momentum of the moment. As you become more familiar with them, you will grow stronger in your self-protection techniques. As we proceed in the book, we will use these three terms, Ethos-Pathos-Logos, to describe important aspects of the manipulator, the persuasive tactics being used, and guide you in your real-time self-protection techniques. Equally important is that we will show you how to apply Ethos, Pathos, and Logos when using the 24 self-protection techniques found in Chapter 6.

Communication:

As we mentioned earlier, communication is the primary tool of manipulation. It is important to have a working knowledge of the ways we communicate. The word "communication " is used to refer to and describe many different aspects of human interaction. Technically, it is the transmitting of information from one person to another with understanding on both ends. "Understanding" is key. Simply sending a message to someone is not communication unless the receiver acknowledges that you've been understood. Accurate or mutual comprehension is optimum, of course. However, we are all familiar with the phrase "break-down in communication," which usually means a lack of clear understanding on one or both ends of the message being sent.

Manipulation:

This book is focused on manipulative tactics used by adults for the sake of self-gain at another adult's expense. This defini-tion can easily fit any number of personality traits, disorders, or behaviors. It could also be that a typically non-calculating person suddenly finds a need to be manipulative. Our purpose in this book is not to focus exclusively on the antisocial personality disorders (APD) such as sociopathy, psychopathy, or narcissism, which use manipulation consistently and nefariously but to iden-tify the most common manipulative tactics used by all of them. We provide resources at the end of the book to give you more background on the different APDs. Our emphasis is on one adult manipulating another adult with the intention of self-gain at the other person's expense. What is important to us is that you can recognize the manipulative tactics and thwart those efforts in real-time with the communication techniques you will learn. Focus on the working definition we use throughout this book: *tactics used by adults on other adults for the sake of self-gain at the other's expense.*

Having said that, let's recognize that as we focus on manipulation, it isn't inherently bad. It's something every human does to get things to go their way, and we learn how to do that very early in life. It's a survival technique almost everyone uses at some point in life. It may be just a little white lie or come in the form of flattery. We may not think of those communications as being manipulative in nature. The type of person and manipulation we are concerned with is the person who will use it in nefarious ways, at any time, targeting an individual with the intent to control and achieve self-aggrandizement.

What is the difference between someone who is being persuasive vs. manipulative? There are two key differences. First is the intent. In manipulative behaviors, the intent is solely to suit the gains of the manipulator with little or no concern for the impact on others. At its most egregious, the manipulator overtly tries to harm the person who is the object or target of exploitation.

The second difference is the ability and or willingness of the recipient to opt-out of the interaction. Persuasion can be compelling, but you can get away, disengage, deny, and disavow the persuader's efforts. A manipulator will be giving you distorted information and/or withholding critical information to serve their personal desire. They make it feel impossible to disengage, make an informed decision or choice.

Some salespeople thrive on the manipulation of information to make the sale. Then we hear them justify the manipulation by saying things like: "People can make their own decision," or "I didn't make her choose that." The same and similar tactics used in these examples are similar to those used by manipulators, whose goal is to exercise control over other people. As in marketing, advertising, sales, and business negotiations, your manipulator may have the goal of controlling your monetary, emotional, psychological, mental, and/or physical decisions and behaviors.

We want to say a quick note about the word "control." There is a difference between control and controlling. Some people feel most comfortable and confident when they are in control of a situation. That may mean that they are literally the person in control of the plans, the procedures, meetings, activities, and how a situation plays out. These people are usually well-intended and considerate of all possible impacts on an event involving other people. They do their research and do their best to be prepared with the intention of having a successful interaction for everyone.

People who are "controlling" are different. These people are most comfortable and satisfied when they are controlling the behavior of other people. Their main goal is to be the person who controls the actions, emotions, and even other people's attitudes. Manipulators fall into this second category. So, as we go along, please accept that even if we use the word "control," we refer to a "controlling" person's mindset and intentions.

EXERCISE:

Practice identifying Ethos, Pathos, and Logos in people you know.

Do you know which method of persuasion is dominant in yourself?

Write it here: _____

What words do you think are most effective to use with:

An Ethos person? _____

A Pathos person? _____

A Logos person? _____

Your biggest challenge will be communicating with the two personalities and methods you know the least! If you are Pathos, speaking with a Pathos person is easy. You need to experiment with the other two and measure your effectiveness by determining whether you could influence and persuade them.

Make your notes here. Which type of personality was it? What did you say? Were you effective? How do you know?

Ethos: _____

_____

_____

_____

_____

Pathos: _____

_____

_____

_____

_____

Logos: _____

_____

_____

_____

_____

2

Why Does the Manipulator Manipulate?

THIS WILL BE a short chapter. The answer to this question has been the focus of many studies, for sure. The information found in these studies can be valuable to a deeper, more academic, and psychological understanding of manipulative behavior. That is not our purpose. This book is designed to give you pragmatic and practical communication techniques for self-protection against manipulation as it is happening in real-time.

A true manipulator does not know how *NOT* to manipulate. It's tough for a normal person to understand. However, it is essential to accept this as a manipulator's default mindset so that you do not become a target. Manipulating for control is the *only* way they know to navigate the world. Efforts to transform or help them will pull you further into their control as they will then use your desire to help as another means to manipulate you. Fun times! Control is like oxygen to them; they can't live without it. As soon as they realize that their efforts have failed to gain control over a person or situation, they vanish, and that's a good thing. Further along in the book, we will talk about making yourself bulletproof to these energy vampires.

So why does the manipulator manipulate people? Why does a manipulator want to control someone's emotions, beliefs, and actions? You have something they want. This could be confidence, looks, status, money, adoration, attention, sex, ethos, etc. You may not even realize what it is until much later. What they are after is truly irrelevant; what is relevant is that you are being exploited.

You may have heard of "love bombing." This is when a manipulator floods their target with compliments, adulation, and gifts. If the target has never been treated that way before, has low self-esteem, or even feels a bit lonely, they can fall *hard* for this tactic. A boss can do this as well with an employee. They may act like you walk on water and sing your praises, telling everyone you're fantastic. BEWARE of this behavior, be cautious of superlative compliments and gushing rhetoric.

Kindness is only temporary until they feel as though you are emotionally tied to them. As good as it may make you feel in the moment, the negative backlash that comes later isn't worth it. It is not easy to find the strength to fight this. It can feel as though you are dehydrated, and this smiling person is handing you a refreshing drink when you are so, so thirsty. What you don't know until it's too late is that your drink is spiked with a poison called *control*.

This is why a manipulator manipulates. So, as we said, this a short chapter because the answer to the question "Why does a manipulator manipulate people?" is one word ... *control*. Period. To find a pattern of control, it will be essential for you to take notes on each situation that occurs. We will remind you of this often, and in Chapter 7, we give you more detail on how to do this.

EXERCISE:

How will you remind yourself that the manipulator ONLY cares about control when they are being charismatic, loving, charming, flattering?

- Put a rubber band on your wrist and snap it?

- Write the word control on the wallpaper of your phone?

- Get a tattoo on the back of your hand?

Write your plan or ideas to remember that control is always the objective here:

_____

_____

_____

_____

_____

_____

_____

_____

_____

_____

3

How Can You Identify a Manipulator?

SPOTTING THE MANIPULATOR can be very difficult. They can be everywhere that humans are found. The manipulator can be anyone! They are difficult to identify because they are so well camouflaged and have no outwardly identifiable physical markings. Manipulators are not restricted to certain locales, climates, social environments, or work settings. They prey on other humans. As a result, you may find them in any place that other humans frequent. No matter how unlikely or unseemly that the place may be, they lie in wait. You won't have to "find" one; they will find you before you ever realize it.

To identify the manipulator, you will need to be a keen observer of behaviors and a critically active listener. You need to understand the manipulator's mindset to interpret your observations and know what you are listening for.

Key indicators of how manipulators think:

They think in terms of win and lose

If someone is winning, they are losing, and they keep score of everything. Win/win does not exist for them. You will notice this in a random conversation where they bring up something from the past that seems minor or odd.

For example, they may say, *"Last time we met the Smiths for dinner, they kept us waiting 30 minutes. So, we are going to take our time this time, and they can wait for us."* You may be thinking, *"that's odd"* or *"who cares"* or *"why does he even remember that?* or *"that's so immature."* Typically it's not worth the debate, so you shrug it off. No matter how insignificant it seems, mark it in your notes.

They show a need for controlling others and situations

They are the puppet master controlling everyone's emotions and actions. It may be part of a strategy to achieve a goal, or it may just be for the sake of feeling smarter and more powerful than others. Think about the cat playing with a mouse that it never kills so that the fun won't stop. If you notice this, mark it in your notes even if it doesn't directly involve you.

They have an insatiable need for adoration and attention

Typically they are charismatic and adept at attracting people. You can usually see them looking to see who's looking at them instead of making genuine eye contact with someone. In fact, make a note of all reflective surfaces and mirrors. Most likely, you will catch them watching themselves; they are like a magpie around shiny objects and just can't resist *"a thousand reflections of their own sweet self."* (Mirror in the Bathroom, English Beat 1980) - Love that song! No matter how minor their behavior seems, mark it in your notes.

They are deeply insecure

They try very hard to hide their insecurity. They may cover it with arrogance, confidence, and bravado, or they could use shyness and helplessness - all means are at their disposal. This insecurity will leak out randomly, so you must pay close attention and take notes! You could be having a wonderful conversation, and they slip in a question or comment that reveals their insecure nature. If you dig deeper, it will go nowhere. They will change the subject if they think they revealed too much. Their deep insecurity is the empty pit inside them, which never fills, hence the "insatiable need" to control. Mark it in your notes when you see it.

They will NEVER allow themselves to show vulnerability

This is difficult to figure out because when another human shows vulnerability, a normal person's instinct is to show sensitivity. In contrast, a manipulator showing vulnerability is a sign of weakness. On the other hand, they will feign vulnerability as a manipulative tactic. Of course, you will want to give the benefit of the doubt to someone who appears vulnerable, and you should. However, if you see any inconsistencies over time, mark those in your notes.

They show feigned empathy to others

They are incapable of truly feeling empathy. If they did feel it, they wouldn't be able to manipulate. Watch for consistency. You may have a relative dying of cancer, and the manipulator may tear up (not real tears, though), hug you, and offer to be of help. One week later, your relative may come up in conversation, and they don't even notice or acknowledge it. Showing empathy at the moment is a common tactic used to cause others to see them as a good and compassionate person. Don't be fooled. They can make it seem quite authentic. If you have any doubts or if it seems overdone or out of character for that person, mark it in your notes!

They ask a lot of questions

One identifiable behavior of a manipulator is that they usually ask many questions if they are going into an unknown situation.

Of course, that's normal for most people so, you have to pay attention to the types of questions. Because the manipulator needs to strategize to control, some of their questions will seem odd, nuanced, or detailed. Even if you suspect and don't know the question's real meaning, mark it in your notes. Eventually, a pattern will show itself.

Now that we have reviewed a bit about the manipulator's mindset, you may realize that this mindset's manifestation comes through infinite types of conversations, behaviors, and circumstances. Are you to go through life suspicious and paranoid? No! That is exactly what this book will help you prevent. While you are learning, you will likely start thinking many people are manipulators who are not. In other words, they may be persuasive to get something to go their way - as we all do - but not necessarily seeking to control another's emotions, beliefs, or actions. Remember our definition of manipulation, " tactics used by adults on other adults for the sake of self-gain at the other's expense."

Over time, with your notes and practice, you will be adept at identifying manipulators. The manipulator will sense that you see through them and avoid you as they have a keen sense of observation and instinctively find the easiest targets.

Identifying manipulative behavior is tricky because it's nuanced, and on the surface, it can seem normal. Nuance is another grand skill of the manipulator. They are constantly refining their abilities to use slightly varied versions of the same behavior to mislead or deceive. Yet, the underlying intentions are the same... controlling someone else. The behaviors WILL form a pattern. So, what should you do? Take notes!

EXERCISE:

To identify the manipulator, you will need to be a keen observer of behaviors and a critically active listener. You need to understand the manipulator's mindset to interpret your observations and listen for specific clues. Taking the identifiers on the next page, apply them to the manipulator, and write one specific example where you witnessed this behavior. This exercise will help you to see the pattern and accept reality.

BEHAVIOR	DATE	DETAILS
Demonstrated Win/Lose Mindset		
Had to control someone/situation		
Needed to be the center of attention		
Showed deep insecurity, jealousy, or envy		
Refused to show weakness when obvious/ appropriate		
Seemed empathetic only to negate it later		
Asked many questions, some seemed odd		

4

What Makes Someone a Good Target for a Manipulator?

THE FOLLOWING CHARACTERISTICS can make you an attractive target for the manipulator:

Accessibility

On a practical level, the manipulator will need to be in contact with the target. They are most dangerous when they have access to you and with regular exposure. This can be in the workplace, at the gym, in a church/temple group meeting, or at home. There is virtually no place to hide from a manipulator. There are so many communication portals in our current world that even physical distance is not a barrier. For most of our social media connections, once you discover that you are the target of a manipulator, you can deny access. They will probably intensify their efforts, so it's easier said than done. There is no way to make sure that you are inaccessible to manipulators, except by going into the woods and living alone, which is not really an option.

Vulnerability

We are all vulnerable in some form or another. When you are the target of the manipulator, you may not be self-aware of your emotional vulnerability. The manipulators are very good at identifying emotional weakness; it is their superpower. Their ability to spot it is much more keen and accurate than a vulnerable individual's ability to recognize it in themselves. It's an awful feeling to reflect on the past and realize how vulnerable you were and recognize the subconscious signals you were sending.

Here are just some examples of transient and universal human moments of vulnerability:

- After a Death
- Pregnancy/Child Birth
- Sickness/Injury
- Divorce or Break Up
- Financial loss
- Being a child and/or dependent
- Traveling in a foreign country
- Being in an unknown situation
- Being concerned about the security of your job
- Being out of a job
- Feeling lonely or being alone
- Being a kid or teenager
- Being a live human facing everyday struggles

As you can see, every human will inevitably be vulnerable in their lifetime. It will be helpful to know there are also personality characteristics that can make you more susceptible. For instance, are you someone who frequently seeks outside approval? Do you lack self-confidence or have low self-esteem? If you have any of these feelings about yourself, a manipulator will sense that, and you could become a target. However, that does not mean that you are immune to being a target if you are confident and self-aware. For a sophisticated and experienced manipulator, they get a bigger thrill from hitting this type of target.

EXERCISE:

On a practical level, the manipulator will need to be in contact with the target. S/he is most dangerous when they have access to you nearby and with regular exposure. This can be in the workplace, at the gym, in a church/temple group meeting, at home, etc.; there is virtually no place that is secure from a manipulator. If you cannot actually separate yourself from the manipulator, you need to know what makes you a good target and try your best to control these things. Ask yourself, How accessible are you?

Never = 1   Sometimes = 2   Always = 3

I respond to every text message immediately _____

I work in a place accessible to the public _____

I always "check in" on Social Media, letting my followers know what I'm doing in real time _____

My Social Media account setting are Public _____

> **Score of 9 or higher:** You are too accessible!
> **Score of 5-8:** You could tighten it up!
> **Score of 4:** Good for you!

How vulnerable are you? Have you recently experienced:

	A Death
	Pregnancy/Child Birth
	Sickness/Injury
	Divorce or Break Up
	Financial Loss
	Financially Dependent on someone
	Traveling in a foreign country
	Being in an unknown situation
	Job instability
	Unemployed
	Feeling lonely or alone
	Being young! Under 25 yrs old

5

Contextual Tactics and the Manipulator

CONTEXT ASKS WHEN, where, and in what environment does the manipulation takes place. Manipulators like to leverage every aspect of that environment. And we mean *every* detail. When and where are the most obvious, of course. They may carefully select the location and time, such as proposing marriage in a particular place that makes it difficult to refuse. They know that you are more likely to give them the answer they want in a more public setting. A public display is an example of how they use the environment to get the answer they want. A common tactic like this is asking an unusual or confusing question when you are with friends or in a business meeting. It may be to humiliate you in front of others or to make you react to a comment unexpectedly and cause embarrassment.

Beyond when and where, however, are such subtle "what" elements of the environment, including lighting, the texture of the surroundings, aroma, other people, time of day, mood, degree of tiredness, and more. Because the context elements are infinite, recognize the coincidences, anything odd or unusual, and mark it in your notes no matter how small or insignificant. We intend to help you turn up the volume on your gut feelings and increase your sensitivity to your surroundings. In other words, operationalize your intuitive process. Don't disregard your instinct or feelings.

Please remember that in addition to the particular communication tactics, the manipulator seeks to use as many of the context elements as possible from moment to moment.

Here are a few examples:

Orchestration - the planning and setup of the context to suit the particular tactic used in deliberate manipulation.

- Proposing an idea or situation so publicly that potential embarrassment prevents logical decision making

- Placing an object in plain view, letting you find it, and then pretending it was a mistake or feigning a lack of awareness

- Letting you overhear something you shouldn't

Orchestration can be anything that uses a combination of the five senses... the point is that *100% of the time,* manipulators are strategizing about *controlling you* - they feel glee when you respond to their set up. For example, you find a bra in the backseat of your boyfriend's car, and the goal is for you to feel jealous and interrogate them. The manipulators' goal was to incite emotions in you, and when you respond accordingly, they are rewarded with a sense of accomplishment. The manipulator may even act embarrassed, shocked, or apologetic to play along while internally feeling victorious and powerful. To them, it's all a game, one which they win through control. It's hard to understand this mindset, let alone accept that someone has it when you yourself don't think that way.

Orchestration takes careful planning to select the particular tactics being used to manipulate a specific person. Imagine an example of what to us seems utterly ridiculous. You are at a meeting at work. Each person has a chair at the conference table. The manipulator has pre-arranged that your chair should be located under hot light or in the sunshine... AND your chair has been adjusted to sit about 6 inches lower than all the other chairs. You naturally feel somewhat uncomfortable, causing you to be less effective in the meeting. Understand the detail and planning required to orchestrate this context. If something like this, similarly odd and unusual, happens to you, mark it in your notes.

Leverage - when the manipulator cannot find a way to orchestrate the context or want to increase their impact, they use such things as the place, timing, or objects at hand to forward the agenda of control. This tactic happens in real-time, often with no overt planning on the part of your manipulator. However, it's important to remember that they are always looking for a way to control your emotions, self-confidence, and/or behavior.

For example:

- Asking/telling you something important when you are hurried or distracted.

- Using a setting where you can't respond, such as making fun of you in front of your boss, friends, neighbors, or even strangers.

- Capitalizing on comments of others to embarrass you in the moment

- Showing up unexpectedly with a contrived excuse

This chapter's point is to alert you that manipulative tactics are often introduced without warning or expectation. Although many of the manipulator's tactics may become familiar and painful to you, they are also capable of both orchestrating and leveraging the context in real-time to control the momentum of the moment. Expect the unexpected and always mark them in your notes.

EXERCISE:

The best way to understand how context is used for manipulation is to notice coincidences or oddly placed objects and note them in the notes section. See the examples below:

Date	Incident
October 2	Went to the concert with Amy and bumped into Byron in the parking lot - he said he was going bowling that night
November 15	Byron had his phone laying on the table face up and got a call from his ex-girlfriend, he left the table to take the call, making a big deal out of it

6

24 Communication Tactics of the Manipulator and Techniques to Outwit Them

MANIPULATORS ARE LIKE good singers. They have their own unique style. Even though the words to a song may be the same, it sure sounds different when sung by Barbra Streisand rather than Rhianna. Tactics used by different manipulators may be relatively the same, but the style they use can vary dramatically.

The **24 tactics** which follow are described in a generic way. You should get familiar with the basic structure of each of them. Your manipulator will truly have their own timing and style of delivery. The subtle differences in approach are exactly what your manipulator uses to confuse you. These timing and delivery differences make it difficult to spot the manipulator in real-time. Their tactics are specific and situational. Manipulators are totally dependent on being able to survey the context of the situation, insert the tactic they planned, and make every effort to control the momentum of the moment. You need to recognize which tactic is being used and have your self-defense technique ready.

The techniques are the specific actions you take when protecting yourself from a manipulative tactic. These include the actual words you can use, the volume and speed at which they are spoken, the non-verbal behavior that accompanies them, and more. Techniques are specific to Ethos, Pathos, and Logos examples. It's important to note that these self-protection methods are aimed at the manipulator. They are intended to have an impact on them and influence their next steps. You must make a careful assessment of techniques you think are more likely to make an impression. This may take some time and careful observation. The notes you have been taking will help you see any trends or patterns of behavior, leading to clues about whether they are more likely to be persuaded, influenced, or impacted by Ethos, Pathos, Logos, or a combination of efforts. Each of the responsive techniques has been carefully designed to strike a particular tone in the manipulator.

These self-protection techniques will help you to react quickly and feel stronger. As you get more comfortable with saying them, it's important to remember that they are designed to impact your manipulator. You may be feeling very emotional (Pathos), but your manipulator may be most effectively influenced by a logical argument or statement (Logos). This means that you must analyze what you think your manipulator is most responsive to instead of what feels more natural for you. If they are moved by emotion, then use the Pathos language. If a logical argument moves them, then you must use the Logos language. If they are moved by hearing the name of a person, place, research study, or other "credible" source, then use the Ethos language.

It is worth repeating that these self-protection techniques and the suggested language are aimed at your manipulator's communication style. Each technique represents a calculated analysis of what the manipulator is most influenced by, not necessarily what makes you feel comfortable in the moment. You are learning how to defend and deflect those attacks that are aimed at you. The goal is to learn how to take control of the momentum of the moment away from the manipulator. When you do that, YOU WIN!

Now, let's review each of the 24 common manipulative tactics and the techniques you can use in real-time as the manipulation is happening.

24 Manipulative Tactics and Corresponding Outwitting Techniques

1. **Ambiguity** - Purposely structuring words/sentences to have multiple meanings or interpretations. Manipulators are good with words, so this tactic is common. They believe that you are not smart enough to detect this tactic. If you feel at all confused during a conversation, feel perfectly comfortable using this self-protection technique.

   Technique: Be persistent about asking clarifying questions. Show your interest in getting the meaning right with the following questions:

   - **Ethos**: *"Your message is important, so I want to be sure I understand it clearly. What do you mean by _____?* Say this with sincerity. Use your normal speed and volume. The facial expression should be plain or a bit inquisitive looking. These words stroke the ego as you are telling them that their message is important.

   - **Pathos**: *"You are always so good about the way you say things, but right now, I feel confused about what you are saying. Please help me understand _____?* Say this with sincerity. You really do want to get clarification of what was just said. Use your normal speed and volume. Facial expression may have a slight smile but not enough as to seem mocking. These words will make them "feel" good while you are still asking for clarity.

   - **Logos**: *"I'm not sure what you mean when you say _____. Would you please clarify that"?* Say this with a direct, non-hesitating tone. Use your normal speed and volume. Try to have direct eye contact to reinforce the seriousness of your interest. Logos language should be said with a serious tone.

Scan the code above with your smartphone camera to watch a short video explanation **Ambiguity** Outwitting Techniques.

This may seem aggressive to the manipulator because they expect you to accept the ambiguity immediately. Often they will use your questioning as a moment to call you a name or question your intelligence. These are, in fact, other tactics. Remain calm and continue to ask those or similar questions until either you get clarification or they change the subject noticing that you have not been fooled.

2. **Apophysis** - a rhetorical or persuasive technique wherein the person brings up a subject by either denying it or contradicting that it should be brought up. For example: "I won't even talk about Judy's crazy hairdo or the ugly clothes she wears, I want to focus on the way she talks to people." Meanwhile, her hair and clothes have been mentioned to make a point. This is a common tactic frequently used by manipulators and politicians. In response to a question, they often say that they will not discuss a subject by mentioning it, reinforcing the controversial feeling surrounding the topic. Of course, they repeat it on purpose to make it part of the conversation.

Technique: To counter this with your manipulator, use humor if you can.

- **Ethos:** Appeal to the ever-present ego by saying something like, *"How clever of you to put it like that."* Say this with a sincere tone. Use a normal volume and speed, and eye contact is okay, but not necessary.

- **Pathos:** *"It's so funny how you say you won't talk about something while you are still talking about it!"* Say this with a slight smile or even a very light bit of laughter. You want to make it clear that you completely get the tactic being used.

- **Logos:** *"So then why would you mention the things that you aren't going to talk about?"* Say this with a direct tone while looking at the person, if possible. If they ask what you mean, repeat what they said and/or repeat what you said. Don't sound angry or like an investigator. Do sound like you clearly heard and understood the tactic. The goal of this technique is for you to let the manipulator know that you recognize what they are doing.

Scan the code above with your smartphone camera to watch a short video explanation **Apophysis** Outwitting Techniques.

3. **Bullying** - Verbal personal attacks that intimidate and non-verbal behavior and/or physical posturing with aggressive energy to cause fear or insecurity.

    Technique: Cease communication immediately, even if you have to hang up or run to the bathroom. The longer you allow someone to hold your attention, the more their contempt for you grows.

    If leaving is not possible, use a technique that we call "rope a dope." You allow yourself to take all the attacking tactics of your manipulator. Don't attempt to refute or argue. If you do, that will only add fuel to the fire and allow your manipulator to think that they have control of your mind, your emotions, and the momentum of the moment. This can be difficult for you to do. Your natural inclination will be to defend yourself.

    Applying this technique requires patience, self-control, and a poker face. When you are convinced that they have worn themselves out, you begin your responses with a strong counter to the points they made. You must find the right time to use this technique because your manipulator may see your rebuttal as a sign of emotional weakness and a willingness to participate.

    So, hold back quietly... wait for the sign that your manipulator is tiring, then come back with a strong voice, tight facial expressions, stiff body language, slightly raised volume, and short sentences that let the manipulator know that you will not tolerate this type of treatment. If you are comfortable, give specific consequences for the next occurrence. A reasonable result could be, "*If you talk to me like that again, this conversation is over.*" If it persists, leave or hang up immediately, or simply stop replying. Continue your *"rope a dope"* technique. By not responding at all, your manipulator may think they controlled your behavior.

So, as we said, allow them to empty their bullying ammunition. When you detect a slow-down in the attack, respond as we suggested. We give you this alternative only to use if you are trapped, like in a car or the shower... remember, they will pick a context for the bullying where you may be unable to leave.

Bullying is not always loud or aggressive. Accomplished manipulators will be able to bully you and make it sound normal. Make no mistake. Bullying is a Pathos act. You know the old saying, " *You can put lipstick on a pig, but it's still a pig.* " We are talking about verbal communication. If there is any physical abuse, seek help immediately. Please see our resource section and learn about how verbal abuse often turns into physical abuse, which is why ceasing communication and/or removing yourself from the location is always recommended.

Scan the code above with your smartphone camera to watch a short video explanation **Bullying** Outwitting Techniques.

4. **Blame** - to hold responsible, find fault with, accuse, or place the responsibility for something on someone else. "*This wouldn't have happened if you had been on time.*" Often, the blame is irrational and misplaced.

Technique: The "*b*roken record" technique can be effective here, repeating the same phrase every time the blame statement is directed at you. You can say:

- **Ethos:** "*I'm surprised that someone with your ability has misinterpreted this. I refuse to accept any blame.*" Say this with a determined sound. Do not hesitate. Say the whole sentence at one time. Keep your volume steady. Eye contact is not necessary, but if you can, look directly at the person.

- **Pathos:** "*I can see that it's easier for you to feel good by falsely blaming me. I refuse to accept any blame.*" Say this with a sense of having just exposed the game. You can recognize what is happening. Use a strong tone, louder than softer - don't shout. It makes you sound desperate. You want to sound decisive.

- **Logos:** "*If you have been able to review all of the parts of this issue, it is hard to accept that you conclude I am responsible. I refuse to accept any blame.*" Say this with a determined tone. You want to sound as though you know all the parts of the issue and that there is no way you are to blame. You could even ask them to review how they came to their conclusion. Your logical, non-emotional demeanor will be quite effective.

It matters little if you say these things fast or slow. You can use your normal daily volume and speed. What matters is the exact repetition of the words. In most cases, don't give the satisfaction of establishing eye contact with this technique. The message you are communicating is that they are not worth your eye contact. Keep repeating the same sentences. What your manipulator wants is to rattle you emotionally. By repeating the same sentences, it will give you control over the momentum of the moment. The goal is to show that you are strong and confident in your conviction and aware of the manipulative tactic. Don't say who is to blame or "*It's not my fault*," as this is a weaker defensive statement. Don't try to justify or explain your view of the issue. It wouldn't matter anyway.

Scan the code above with your smartphone camera to watch a short video explanation **Blame** Outwitting Techniques.

5. **Calculation and Planning** - events occur resulting from calculation and planning but are perceived by the target to be a coincidence. This may include manipulating the physical environment and knowingly using objects or locations to incite emotion. It will help you to re-read the "Context" portion in Chapter 5.

Manipulators are keen and strategic calculators and planners. If there is a claim by the manipulator that all the plans have been made, not to worry, everything is under control; your awareness should be heightened. This can be about tiny and seemingly inconsequential matters, or it can be about serious and major concerns. The key here is that your red flag is ready to fly; your caution/alert button is always flashing.

Technique: In these situations, ask a lot of questions. These should be questions of clarification. The manipulator may simply lie. They may challenge you for why you want to know. They may accuse you of being too cautious or too inquisitive or too suspicious or too controlling! Don't let that bother you. Those comments are only meant to make you feel inferior, stupid, or paranoid. They are part of this manipulative tactic. Be sure that you don't exhibit any of those characteristics but are still recognizing the tactic being used. Stick to your guns and continue to ask questions of clarification. However, you may not be getting the whole truth no matter what you ask or how you ask it.

You can say this:

- **Ethos:** *This all sounds well thought out. Who made that plan?"* Say this with a calm and direct volume and speed. Eye contact is not important here but can't hurt. You should sound confident and deliberate in wanting that information.

- **Pathos:** *"This sounds like a strange way to do this. How come?"* Say this with a quizzical sound. Don't be accusatory, just inquisitive. You can use a bit of a smile as though the whole thing sounds odd.

- **Logos:** *"What options are there?"* Say this just like it is written here ... short and direct. Keep your volume and speed the same all the way through the question. If needed, repeat the same question.

Try not to sound accusatory. Ask the questions in a simple, relatively non-emotional manner. If you sound challenging, that will stir a new set of tactics on the manipulator's part. If you begin to have doubts that the manipulator is still calculating or think that you are acting too suspicious, STOP THINKING LIKE THAT! When dealing with these sorts of people, it's better to be safe than sorry.

Scan the code above with your smartphone camera to watch a short video explanation **Calculation and Planning** Outwitting Techniques.

6. **Changing the Subject** - usually, the manipulator is pivoting from a topic that makes them uncomfortable or one with guarded information they don't want to share. They will often change to a subject that the target will latch onto and be eager to talk about. This is done to distract. This tactic is often used in collaboration with other manipulative tactics.

Technique: Your listening skills and your ability to stay focused without getting triggered by their attempt to distract you using emotional references or outbursts will be valuable here. Stay on track by not responding to the subject change. This can feel awkward and even rude; however, it's effective in sending the signal that you are aware of the manipulative tactic. In a calm, non-accusatory voice, you can say:

- **Ethos:** *"I admire your ability to talk about more than one thing at a time, but would you please stay on topic A before we move to topic B?"* Say this with a clear and confident sound. Use a steady volume and speed. Complete the sentences with no hesitation.

- **Pathos:** *"Wait a minute. I feel a little lost. Could we stay on topic A before moving to topic B?"* Say this with the self-confidence that you have just identified a manipulative tactic and control the momentum of the moment. You can use a quizzical tone. Facial expressions can even show a slight smile. Be sure not to sound mocking here, though.

- **Logos:** *"This conversation will be more effective if we complete topic A before changing to topic B."* Say this with a steady and determined tone, volume, and speed. You are making a statement. You are not asking a question.

Any response like these will signal that you are paying attention and are clarifying any confusion or change of subject. The point is not to be accusatory. Rather, you recognize the attempt to change the topic. Be prepared once you have clearly established your attention and identification of the tactic, that it may immediately evolve into another tactic like Blame. If it does, give yourself some credit, you are controlling the momentum of the moment.

Scan the code above with your smartphone camera to watch a short video explanation **Changing the Subject** Outwitting Techniques.

7. **Conflation** - mixing two distinct thoughts/events as if they were one. This, of course, is a favorite technique of all manipulators. They believe that you cannot follow or keep up with their clever manipulation of language and ideas. This tactic can easily be confused with the tactic of Changing the

Subject. In fact, manipulators are adept at merging these two tactics. In situations like this, you will need your good listening skills. One key to identifying the difference between the two tactics is that the Conflation tactic will have related topics. They may be names, places, or events that are merged into the conversation. If you are confused about which tactic is being used, don't be afraid to act on the one you are most confident about and respond accordingly, using either the words "conflation" or "change of subject."

Technique: Ignore the conflation and continue to focus only on one subject, or point out the conflation and insist on addressing each thing separately.

Here are some things you can say:

- **Ethos:** *"Can you help me understand how X and Y are related?"* Say this with a tone of sincerely wanting to get guidance or clarification. Use a steady, firm sound. Volume and speed can be normal. Don't sound challenging, even though it may be tempting. Sound as though you are thirsty for information from the fountain of knowledge ... omg! But that's how Ethos manipulators see themselves.

- **Pathos:** *"I feel confused and unable to respond when you conflate X and Z. Let's just talk about X first, then Z separately."* Say this with a bit of anxiety... not too much. You don't want to sound weak. You want to sound as though you recognize that different subjects are being conflated and would like clarification before proceeding.

- **Logos:** *"It will be more efficient if we just focus on X right now, rather than conflating it with Z."* Say this directly. Do not hesitate. Use a steady delivery. Keep your volume and speed constant and normal. You want this to sound a bit like advice without being pushy. Your strength will cause the manipulator to wonder if the tactic has worked. It hasn't. You win!

You don't need to say it as if you caught them in a tactic, just be matter of fact.

If the moment allows it, use direct eye contact when you say it. If eye contact is not possible or too difficult for you, simply use those words. Doing this is evidence that you are not being fooled and are expecting a direct response.

Scan the code above with your smartphone camera to watch a short video explanation **Conflation** Outwitting Techniques.

8. **Creating Self-Doubt** - this tactic is used by a manipulator insidiously, often through non-verbal disapproval or verbally packaged as a joke. This is usually executed in small ways over time and is often combined with other tactics. The purpose is to cause you to doubt or disbelieve what your instincts or evidence tells you.

   Technique: Pay attention. That is, if you suspect that this tactic is being used, give careful attention to the details of the interaction or agreement. Be sure to prepare yourself by reinforcing your confidence in your understanding and conviction about the issue. If something seems counter to your understanding, you can say this:

- **Ethos:** *"Your credibility fails with me when you try to create self-doubt in me by* _____. *(state specific behavior/ words)."* Say this with conviction unless your manipulator has tried to make a joke about it. Then, say this with as much humor or sarcasm as the manipulator gave it. Your aim here is to make them realize that you are calling them out for this tactic. Don't be shy with this technique. It is a direct attempt to identify the tactic.

- **Pathos:** *"Do you ever find it annoying when someone says things that make you doubt your own beliefs about something?"* Then say nothing, no matter how long the silence lasts, make sure the manipulator is the next one to speak. Say this with a curious tone. Don't sound accusatory until the denials get so constant that you have to make a direct analysis of what was said. You can also do this with the same amount of humor as the manipulator used.

- **Logos:** *"Your signals (words) of disapproval are ineffective."* Say this with certainty that you heard what was said and/or observed the nonverbal signals. Your sound of self-confidence will likely evoke a bit of annoyance. So what? Stick to it, and soon, they will change the subject altogether, noticing that you have spotted the tactic.

These responses will shift the attention to your manipulator and cause them some self-doubt; however, you must remain quiet and let them be the one to speak next, so wait! Your volume, speed, facial expression, and body language can all be matter of fact. Your lack of emotional expression will help to displace the effort to create self-doubt. If you need confirmation of your suspicions or your interpretation of things, your notes will be helpful here.

Scan the code above with your smartphone camera to watch a short video explanation **Creating Self-Doubt** Outwitting Techniques.

9. **Dictating Feelings** - interpreting your feelings and telling you how you feel. This can be done with very loving tones as though they are really concerned about your welfare. "*Oh, honey, I'm sure you must feel very sad about all this. I want to be helpful.*" It can also be done in a matter of fact way as if they are simply reminding you of something. "*Remember how furious you were when _____ happened.*" You may have been only slightly annoyed.

    Technique: Both of these reasons for using this tactic are fake. Your manipulator has assessed you to be vulnerable, oblivious to your own feelings, and incapable of properly expressing your emotions. No matter what, never let your manipulator tell you how you are feeling. You own your thoughts, opinions, and beliefs. They are yours, and you will decide what they are and how to express them. You can say this:

    - **Ethos:** "*I know that you are good at assessing feelings and attitudes, but in this case, what I actually feel is _____.*" Say this with both an attitude and sound of conviction. On the one hand, you are stroking the ego while at the same time stating and showing your own sense of self-confidence. Your speed and volume should stay consistent throughout.

- **Pathos:** *"For goodness sake, you may feel like that, but I actually feel _____."* Say this with a sound of amazement that someone could feel that way. You can also use a face that shows a bit of surprise that they carry such an inaccurate assessment of your feeling while having a clear emotion and attitude about the issue.

- **Logos:** *"That is incorrect. My actual feelings are _____."* Say this without hesitation and with a matter of fact tone. Keep your speed and volume consistent with the sound of determination to correct what your manipulator has said. If you do this more than once, you will probably cause them to abandon this tactic. You win!

Don't be apathetic about making these corrections in real-time. It's imperative to put the manipulator on notice so that you won't be manipulated by a single word.

Scan the code above with your smartphone camera to watch a short video explanation **Dictating Feelings** Outwitting Techniques.

10. **Gaslighting** - to cause a person to doubt their reality or sanity through the use of psychological manipulation by denying and/or redefining reality. The manipulator insists that something isn't true or didn't happen even though you may have witnessed it. If you have this experience, be sure to mark it in your notes. You will soon see a pattern of consistent attempts to deny the reality of what you know you

experienced or thought. You may be able to witness gaslighting happening to someone else before you identify it in your life. We often see examples of this with political figures who constantly insist that something is not what it seems. The public's understanding of the situation is wrong, even when you may have experienced the reality yourself. This is an insidious tactic. It takes place over time and when you may least expect it. To help you identify gaslighting, listen for particular phrases like:

"Don't be so sensitive."
"You're just paranoid."
"You're talking like a crazy person."
"You must be the only person who thinks that."
"Your memory is really failing you these days."

Technique: Stay calm! Any emotional outburst will be used to blame you for being out of control. Don't dig in your heels and get defensive or aggressive. In a calm voice, let your manipulator know that you and they seem to see things differently. Identify where those differences may be and ask for their help in clarifying. Then, don't forget to mark it in your notes. This pattern will show itself with careful record keeping. In real-time, you can say:

- **Ethos:** "*That's interesting. I don't recall it like that. I wonder why you do?*" Say this with the tone and attitude of quizzical disbelief, as though that's not the way you recall things. If possible, look right at the manipulator. Make it clear that you are not accepting what was said.

- **Pathos:** "*Come on, that's not what happened. Where did you get that idea?*" Say this with the sound of open disbelief and astonishment. You can raise your volume slightly to indicate your surprise. No need to make eye contact. That would give this particular response too much credibility.

- **Logos:** *"Do you have facts/evidence for what you are saying?"* Insist on the facts. Don't be shy. Be confident.

Gaslighting is an effort to wear you down, thereby causing you to believe that your perception or understanding is not correct. It happens over time to avoid being too obvious. Each time you think you may be being gaslighted, be sure to mark it in your notes. If they talk over you and/or interrupt you, keep talking and finish your thought, don't let them take control of the momentum. This is a time when those notes you have been taking will come in handy.

Scan the code above with your smartphone camera to watch a short video explanation **Gaslighting** Outwitting Techniques.

11. **Grooming (Love bombing)** - Kindness, romance, flattery, adoration, devotion, fairytale, and fun activities all with a hidden agenda to gain control over the target. The term "grooming" is often heard when describing a pedophile who will use this tactic to attract and influence an unknowing young person who is eventually taken advantage of in various ways. It's not uncommon for the same tactic to be used with adults, sometimes referred to as love bombing. Unlike some other more annoying, embarrassing, or hurtful tactics, this one can feel great. Why not? When comments and treatments are pleasant and rewarding, it feels good. Until... it doesn't. There comes a time when your manipulator pulls the plug on niceness and expects you to behave or communicate

in a way that may be uncomfortable to you. You'll wonder if you're wrong. This person has been so nice, fun, and pleasant. If you suspect you are being love-bombed, mark it in your notes, and over time the pattern will appear.

Technique: Be very careful. If you are asked to do or say or behave in a way that is not comfortable for you, be sure to mark it in your notes. Of course, you always have free will and can trust your instinct, intuition, and refuse. This can be difficult because love bombing is intended to get you to lower your defenses. So, always receive the comments or behaviors neutrally, avoid fawning, or giving the manipulator too much affirmation that it is working. We truly know that this may be a challenge because the love bombing feels good. If you suspect you are being love-bombed as you are authenticating and evaluating things, you can say this:

- **Ethos:** *"When I hear someone like you say (do) these kinds of things, it makes me wonder if you are really sincere."* Say this with a sense of respect. Do make direct eye contact. Use a soft and non-threatening volume. Do not hesitate as you say these words. Say them all in one sentence. It will make you sound stronger.

- **Pathos:** *"You seem like such a nice person that, at times, it feels a little uncomfortable for me."* Say this with some discomfort. Do not make eye contact. You can hesitate a little bit as you say these words. Create the effect of being a little confused about how someone can be so nice all the time.

- **Logos:** *"Can anything or anyone be as positive (perfect) as you make it sound?"* Say this with a bit of skepticism. Use a steady volume and speed. Make direct eye contact and wait for a reply. If you don't get one, repeat the question.

Love bombing/grooming can be complicated to detect, especially if your manipulator is more likely to use other tactics.

The whole goal is to lower your defenses and start to feel comfortable with that person. It can go on for a long time, even years. We have heard many stories of manipulative tactics that are used in conjunction with love bombing. You will have to lower your emotion flag and raise your suspicion flag.

Scan the code above with your smartphone camera to watch a short video explanation **Grooming** (Love-Bombing) Outwitting Techniques.

12. **Hurt and Rescue (Munchausen Syndrome)** - This tactic can border on being dangerous. The manipulator will create a calculated crisis. It can be:

- physical, related to your health

- psychological, causing deep worry

- situational, like something going wrong with a carefully planned activity

This tactic is used to incite fearful emotions in the target so that the manipulator can then be the hero and rescue the target or solve the problem. Sadly, this tactic has all too often been identified as a tool used by adults on children. It is also common with adults using it against a sensitive person who truly cares for other people's well-being. Your manipulator will know this about you. They will create situations or environments that will draw your attention. Then, they will appear just in time to save the day. Each time, your manipulator will reinforce their role as the savior, hero, or problem solver. That is the identifying factor for you.

Technique: First of all, be sure you can clearly identify this tactic. It will be repeated in different ways. The notes you have been keeping will remind you of various times when you noticed something odd. If you recognize this tactic, avoid receiving the help, solution, or answer from the manipulator who is causing the problem to begin with!! Instead, call out your manipulator for using it. If they realize that you have discovered their effort, they will quickly pivot to another tactic. You can say this:

- **Ethos:** *"You are so considerate to offer your help, and even if it turns out to be a significant challenge, I can handle it."* Say this with confidence. Avoid sounding uncertain or nervous. Use strong volume and steady speed. The facial expression should be solid and bordering on stern and determined.

- **Pathos:** *"I appreciate the offer; however, I will handle this one myself."* Say these things with a straight face and a confident, almost upbeat tone and volume. You want to give the impression of being in control and capable. Knowing that you have uncovered the tactic, it may make you feel good to say, *"Thanks, for offering to help, though."*

- **Logos:** *"I know how to correct the issue. I'll take it from here."* Say this with a calm, confident tone, even volume, and speed. You can sound a bit perfunctory, almost dismissive sounding.

We want to repeat that this can be a dangerous tactic. This is especially true if your manipulator is creating some sort of physically harmful situation. If your instincts tell you that something is not right and something harmful could result, get away from the scene, or call the authorities for help. Even if it turns out to be a false alarm, you will feel better asking for outside help and not allowing your manipulator to take the credit. If they tried it once, they might surely try it again. Be careful and always mark this in your notes.

Scan the code above with your smartphone camera to watch a short video explanation **Hurt and Rescue** Outwitting Techniques.

13. **Invalidation -** What is most important to the manipulator when using this tactic is minimizing your opinions, feelings, and perceptions, demonstrating disregard for you non-verbally and verbally. This one is tricky because it usually involves changing the subject or ignoring something that is of value to you. It's another subtle way to let you know you are not important. Many of these manipulative tactics are used in tandem. This is one of them. It is often combined with #8 *Creating Self Doubt* or #6 *Changing The Subject.* Your best overall defense for this and other tactics is to build your skill of having a strong and controlled mindset. If you can learn to control your thoughts, you will be much stronger when using these self-protection techniques. Be sure to spend some time reading Chapter 7 *Self Protection Skills* about your mindset's importance.

Technique: It's best to make an "I" statement, short and strong, to put the manipulator on notice that you see what's happening as soon as you recognize the tactic. The longer you wait, the more it reinforces the manipulator's efforts to make you feel invalidated and worthless.

- **Ethos:** *"When you invalidate my feelings, you lose credibility."* Say this with a deliberate tone. Don't hesitate or indicate that you are confused or shy. Use your normal speed and volume.

- **Pathos:** *"I won't continue this conversation without you acknowledging my feelings."* Say this with determination and a bit of challenge. You are calling it out. Give yourself credit for having the strength to say this with conviction. Use a strong and steady volume and speed. Establishing eye contact is good if you can do it.

- **Logos:** *"I am finding this conversation unproductive. When you are prepared to discuss without minimizing, disparaging, or disregarding me, let me know."* Good for you if you can say this with strength and commitment. Use a slightly louder volume than normal. The speed of speaking can be normal but be sure to avoid hesitation. Say it without allowing any interruption.

It's important to say these things with a strong, deliberate, confident voice. Don't hesitate or stop in the middle of the sentence. Making eye contact is helpful if you can use it comfortably. Then FOLLOW THROUGH by ending the conversation if they don't acknowledge what you said. Remember, this tactic is often used in combination with other tactics. You will need to become familiar with the tactics we have identified and deal with each accordingly. In this case, stick to your guns. If you do not get recognition, cease the conversation if you can do it safely.

Scan the code above with your smartphone camera to watch a short video explanation **Invalidation** Outwitting Techniques.

14. **Irony** - meaning anything except the literal meaning of the word, often used as humor but intended to embarrass. Manipulators are often quite adept at the use of language. It is the primary weapon in manipulative tactics. This method is frequently used to humiliate you and make you look naive.

Technique: Don't show embarrassment. Ignore the irony and respond to the words literally - at face value. To protect yourself, if you don't understand the use of a word or it's being used in some unusual way, be careful. It could be a test to evaluate your comfort with language and its usage. Use these words to protect yourself:

- **Ethos:** *"I know you are good with words, but you said that in an awkward way."* Say this with a calm but deliberate tone. You are calling them out with this technique. Use a normal speed and volume. The facial expression should be stern and directed toward them if possible.

- **Pathos:** *"I know you mean that as humor, but it's actually quite rude and not funny."* Say this with a somewhat disgusted tone. Use a steady delivery with firm volume and speed. The facial expression should show disappointment.

- **Logos:** *"That is an odd way to say that. What do you really mean?"* Say this with a bit of disappointment and wonder what the logic and relevance is to the topic. Use direct facial expression and eye contact with the manipulator. A non-stop delivery indicates a clear intent of your statement. Say all of these words with a strong, confident voice that communicates you recognize the tactic and do not appreciate it. Direct eye contact can be helpful here, as well.

Scan the code above with your smartphone camera to watch a short video explanation **Irony** Outwitting Techniques.

15. **Leveraging Others** - using your relationship with others to manipulate you either overtly or covertly. *"Everyone thinks you're crazy!"* or, *"Even your mother thinks you're a slob."* Normally, the things that are said are either not true or only partially true and reinterpreted to fit the attempt to mislead, embarrass, or conflate with a different tactic or topic. Often the third party is not aware that they are being used.

Technique: You just can't care about this. It's hard because the third party seems innocent and is convincing. Of course, at some point, you must check with the third party to confirm the truth of what was said. At the moment it is being used, you can say:

- **Ethos:** *"Isn't your opinion sufficient without the need to repeat the opinion of other people?"* Say this with a bit of both surprise and sarcasm of your own. You can show a small smile while making a face of polite challenge. You are not trying to be humorous but are slightly surprised that they have consulted someone else on this topic.

- **Pathos:** *"Where the heck did you get that idea?"* Say this with polite surprise. Use a somewhat louder volume and faster speed. The facial expression should have raised eyebrows and a slight smile.

- **Logos:** *"When/where did you hear that?"* Say this with a sense of wonder and the surprise of honest investigation for the facts. Don't be accusatory, or you make an honest person feel uncomfortable.

Say this with the deliberate sound of wanting validation of what was just said. You are asking for proof or documentation to support said the comment. Don't sound accusatory, just seeking accuracy of the statement made.

If you choose to say these words, do so with strength and confidence, normal volume, and no direct eye contact. You want to show basic disbelief in the statements. Ideally, ignore the statements, remembering to control your non-verbal reaction (poker face). You will know you are succeeding when the statements escalate or get defensive.

Scan the code above with your smartphone camera to watch a short video explanation **Leveraging Others** Outwitting Techniques.

16. **Name-Calling** - comparison to people you despise *"You're just like your father"* or the good old fashioned stand by, *"You're such a bitch/dick!"* Yes, we know that this is a childish tactic, frequently heard in grade school. In those settings, remember what we learned to reply? *"Sticks and stones may break my bones, but names will never hurt me."* Well, name-calling is hurtful, and that is why manipulators use this tactic. This method is often used by manipulators who do not have a full toolbox of tactics from which to choose. Of course, it will appear when the manipulator is out of patience, irritated, or at a loss because other tactics have been unsuccessful. Most commonly, it is used in combination with other tactics.

Technique: When the latter is the case, isolate this name-calling tactic as childish. Don't be shy about it. No matter whether you say it with Ethos, Pathos, or Logos, do not hesitate. You are creating and delivering a message of determination.

- **Ethos** - *"I'm surprised someone with your intellect would stoop to name-calling, it seems beneath you. The next time you call me a name, this conversation will end abruptly."* Say this with determination based on having identified the tactic. Use a strong volume and speed. Make eye contact if possible. If needed, repeat the same sentence. If it continues, leave or hang up if possible.

- **Pathos** - *"You must be feeling bad about yourself to use name-calling to make your point. The next time you call me a name, this conversation is over."* Say this with determination. Use a strong volume and speed. Do not hesitate. Say the entire thing at one time. If it is repeated, stop talking, hang up, or leave if possible.

- **Logos** - *"It's very ineffective to use name-calling as an adult. The next time you call me a name, this conversation* *will end immediately.*" If it is repeated, you're done! Stop talking and leave if possible.

Tolerating this in any way will only increase the behavior. Be swift and consistent. You must use a strong, moderately loud volume and deliberate wording with no hesitation or tolerance of this tactic. You are communicating that you are taking charge of the momentum of the moment. There is a great cost to tolerating this tactic; it is a demonstration of contempt. When you allow it, the manipulator's contempt for you grows exponentially and can move toward physical violence.

Scan the code above with your smartphone camera to watch a short video explanation **Name-Calling** Outwitting Techniques.

17. **Non-Verbal Disapproval and Approval -** facial expression and paralanguage are common and are often used with most tactics. Paralanguage uses small grunts or snickers that are not actually words but carry meaning and emphasis to what has been said. In fact, when you mark things in your notes, be sure to record the non-verbal and paralanguage as well. Some manipulators use this tactic with almost every other tactic they employ. Many manipulators are finely tuned to this tactic. They can use physical proximity or facial expressions, even micro expressions (those tiny, almost unseen movements) with the intention that only you will see. Sometimes they will want these tiny expressions to be seen by someone else as a way to embarrass you.

Technique: Although it's challenging, ignore non-verbal communication. Focus on the value of the words only, and refuse to accept the subtext. Sometimes they are sending these messages while you are engaged with another in conversation. Turn your body away or change locations to shut off their non-verbal messages of disapproval. YOUR non-verbal behavior can show that two can play that game. You can be subtle about it. There is no need to be blatantly obvious UNLESS, at that moment, you decide that such action will give you strength and control. In that case, take control of the momentum of that moment by showing it. You do not need to say anything when dealing with this tactic. Basically, show it no attention. Remember to mark it in your notes.

Scan the code above with your smartphone camera to watch a short video explanation **Non-Verbal/Disapproval** Outwitting Techniques.

18. **Public Humiliation** - using the threat of embarrassing you to control you. Sharing information, typically gained in confidence, about personal insecurity that will knowingly hurt you deeply. This tactic can take one of two directions. Your manipulator may choose to say or do something that others will see with the intent of embarrassing you in a very public way. Or they may share inaccurate information privately, quietly, so no one else is aware of it intending to make you say or act in a way that may embarrass you publicly.

Technique: This is often the manipulator's BIGGEST weapon. The only way to diffuse it is to REFUSE IT. Prepare your mindset for this tactic and be ready to refuse humiliation no matter what. Now, we know that it is easier said than done. Sometimes private, embarrassing information is revealed under the umbrella of humor by the manipulator. Feeling embarrassed plays into their hands and empowers them. They will use this technique to test where your biggest vulnerabilities lie and use that information in future manipulation. You must diffuse it by having no response.

Demonstrate that you have a mindset of self-worth, self-confidence, and recognition that everyone has aspects of their personality or life story that could humiliate them. It's a human condition. The less attention you give to these efforts, the more successful you will be. You may feel humiliated internally; however, it's important not to show it externally. The manipulator is hoping that you will express that embarrassment publicly. If you have strengthened your mindset to be prepared for this tactic, you will control your reactions and send a message to your manipulator that this tactic will not work with you. Make notes later about how you felt and what happened to motivate yourself to get away permanently from this person. To prevent this sort of tactic from having any power, avoid disclosing personal information that might encourage them.

Scan the code above with your smartphone camera to watch a short video explanation **Public Humiliation** Outwitting Techniques.

19. **Reframing a Past Event -** the manipulator twists and distorts the facts of past events to benefit their agenda. This often occurs with storytelling, which frames the story's elements in how the manipulator wants you to feel and/or be perceived by others. This tactic will contain some true elements added to provide some authenticity and familiarity to the story. The hope is that you will not recognize the reframing when it is woven into the story. Reframing may sound a lot like Gaslighting, but the tactic is more specific. Gaslighting is used to refer to general items or situations. It may be helpful to go back and review tactic 10 about Gaslighting.

Technique: As you already know, you will have to be listening carefully whenever the manipulator is speaking. When it is clear to you that the manipulator is incorrectly restating a past event, allow the restatement to finish. Don't interrupt. This will take some practice and self-control on your part. You will want to respond immediately. If you do jump in before the comment is complete, you will be accused of being rude or worse. When the statement is complete, immediately begin your response by being direct. Here are some things that you can say:

- **Ethos:** *"Interesting. You are normally so accurate with details. This time, however, your recollection is not right. Actually, what happened is _____."* Say this without hesitation. Use your normal speed and volume. Eye contact will strengthen your resolve and show the manipulator that you mean business.

- **Pathos:** *"That's not at all the way I recall that event. I'm surprised at you."* Say this with a bit of surprise in your voice. Volume can be a bit faster than normal, and speed can be a bit faster. Eyebrows can be a bit raised with a look of surprise.

- **Logos:** *"I know you like to be accurate, so I must correct the statement about _____"* Say this as though you have the intent of correcting a misinterpretation of the facts. Don't sound accusatory. Do sound confident. Say the whole sentence and stop.

These responses may stir more conversation filled with reframing or conflation with other thoughts. Be careful that if you are compelled to say more, you will be playing into the hands of the manipulator and provide great fodder for them to continue. This is a situation where less is more. Keep it short and to the point. Your objective here is to correct an inaccuracy of the statement.

Scan the code above with your smartphone camera to watch a short video explanation **Reframing a Past Event** Outwitting Techniques.

20. **Repetition of False Information -** confidently repeating false facts until you accept it. This is a favorite and famous tactic used by many people, companies, politicians, and advertisers. Take notice of how many times you see or hear the same commercials on radio or television. How many times have you heard politicians say the same words? Repetition is the tool used to get you and others to accept false information as fact. It's effective if you are not diligent in rejecting the claim every time. Manipulators know that repetition works even if the facts are not accurate.

Technique: A way to handle this is to embrace the false information with humor/sarcasm and make a joke of it by adding your own exaggeration to the narrative. You will come across as confident and resilient. You can say:

- **Ethos:** *"Because your credibility is at risk, I simply must correct what you keep repeating about _____. The truth is _____."* Say this with the tone of being helpful to a person who has made a factual error. Use normal volume and speed with no hesitation. Eye contact will strengthen your message.

- **Pathos:** *"Because you keep repeating _____, you must feel strongly about it: however, the truth is _____. Your repetitive statements will not change the way I feel."* Say this with determination. If you can, add a small smile to emphasize the weakness of repeating something that is not true.

- **Logos:** *"Accuracy is essential and your repetitive claim of _____ is incorrect. The fact is _____."* Say this in a short statement. Use strong volume and speed. Do not hesitate. You are expressing the importance of accuracy and determination.

If you feel the need to clear the record, correct the facts, protect your reputation, or otherwise bring truth and accuracy to the moment, do it with confidence and clarity.

This response by you will often lead them to lie or lead to a different tactic. You need to listen carefully and be sure of your own comments before you respond. It is better to be brief with your response as you have learned manipulators thrive on engaging you.

Scan the code above with your smartphone camera to watch a short video explanation **Repetition of False Information** Outwitting Techniques.

21. **Sarcasm -** using words to inflict pain, embarrassment, or to show a form of disrespect. This tactic is often used with irony or as part of other tactics. Interestingly, sarcasm can be quite funny when used to identify a universal emotion or experience; however, it can be hurtful when used toward someone personally.

Technique: You have a couple of choices as to how to react to this tactic. You can interpret the comment literally instead of the hidden meaning. Even if you know this is sarcasm, simply show no reaction. Sarcasm only works if you react to its intended use. You might simply change the subject. Another way to deal with sarcasm is by labeling it and commenting on it. You can say:

- **Ethos:** "*I know you are well educated, but what you just said could be interpreted as hurtful and immature.*" Say this with a tone of disappointment. Use a softer volume and a slower speed as though you are talking to someone who needs guidance.

- **Pathos:** "*You have a great sense of humor, but sarcasm can make other people feel bad. Why are you saying that?*" Say this with a tone of soft shaming like an older grandparent advising a maturing teenager. You are identifying the sarcasm with a polite chastisement and a smile.

- **Logos:** " *That makes no sense.*" Then walk away, hang up, or stop talking.

Remember that sarcasm can be used for humor or hurt. Be sure that it is personal and act accordingly. Most important is recognizing that it is a tactic designed to control your ability to function or follow the conversation. Sarcasm is often used as a test to identify your sensitivities. If you suspect that it is being used on you, mark it in your notes. It will surely be used again.

Scan the code above with your smartphone camera to watch a short video explanation **Sarcasm** Outwitting Techniques.

22. **Use of a Surrogate -** This is the use of another person to manipulate you. This tactic is intended to take responsibility away from the manipulator. The surrogate is a tool to convey news. They may not be saying anything related directly to the manipulator. In fact, the surrogate may not even realize that they are being used. The message is so well crafted that it may refer to something that impacts you more indirectly.

Technique - When the manipulator needs to enlist the help of a surrogate, you should realize that YOU are stronger than you think. Typically this is necessary when the manipulator cannot exploit you by themselves, so they use and control people who influence you to do their bidding. The key is to recognize this is happening and, if possible, tell the surrogate politely what you think is happening. Urge the surrogate to protect themselves unless you think they will disclose your warning to the manipulator.

Say to the surrogate:

- **Ethos:** *"Because I always appreciate your opinion/ thoughts, I'll give your comments serious consideration."* Say this with sincerity. Use a soft volume and an average speed. Facial expressions should be serious but not challenging or suspicious. Your mindset should be one of caution. Commit to investigating this later.

- **Pathos:** *"I feel as though M is using our relationship to influence how I feel. I prefer to gauge my own feelings."* Say this with a slight smile, but the sound of determination and discovery. That is, you have identified this tactic and don't appreciate it.

- **Logos:** *"Thank you for your assessment. I'll draw my conclusions/opinions based on evidence rather than influence from others."* Then, there is the simple response of *"okay"* as you move on and see it for what it is. Pick your battles. The surrogate may be very loyal to the manipulator, so it may be best to go with a simple response. If they are unaware of being used, you don't want to waste energy or risk the friendship by engaging it.

Scan the code above with your smartphone camera to watch a short video explanation **Use of Surrogate** Outwitting Techniques.

23. **Word Use, Choice, and Inflection -** Manipulators are masters of using words and their delivery to embarrass, intimidate, and confuse you. This is one of the most pervasive and insidious tactics of all. These words and delivery style are designed to make you feel shame, to embarrass you, irritate you, confuse you, make fun of you, and make you feel as though there is something wrong with you or that you did something wrong. This tactic is used to stir a heightened emotional reaction.

Technique - As noted, this tactic is very popular with manipulators. Pay close attention to tone, timing, volume, speed, and word choice. If you find yourself feeling icky and awful after a communication, this technique is most likely used. It can often be veiled in compliments. Being a good listener is important here. If nervousness or something else is bothering you, try using an audio recorder. It will help you dissect this later. If you can't do that, make some notes right after the incident. Write down the specific words that hurt and why. This will help you identify the pattern sooner and get away. Depending on the situation, you could say:

- **Ethos:** *"You have a way with words, but I didn't understand what you meant when you said _____."* Say this with a polite sound. You are respectful while asking a legitimate question.

- **Pathos:** *"You must feel pretty bad about yourself to use language like that."* Say this with a bit of anger, disgust, surprise, or disappointment. Don't hesitate when you say it. Use a short sentence. Use substantial volume and constant speed. Your facial expression should be stoic, showing that you clearly understand what was said.

- **Logos:** *"You sound irrational and ineffective when you use that tone and those words."* Then, stop talking. If you notice no change, repeat it. You are making a logical statement of your feeling and attitude toward such language. It will show the strength and self-confidence you have.

Scan the code above with your smartphone camera to watch a short video explanation **Word Use, Choice, Inflection** Outwitting Techniques.

24. **Non-Verbal Communication -** We would be totally remiss if we left out non-verbal communication tactics! Have you heard of micro expressions? They are facial expressions that are so quick (half a second) that they are recognized by your subconscious rather than your conscious mind most of the time. These expressions can't be faked. Think of them as a quick reveal of your manipulator's true motivation.

It takes a lot of focus and practice to see these expressions. You will likely feel uneasy after the exchange because of the disconnect between what your sub-conscious and conscious mind heard. Suppose you have a long term relationship with a manipulator. In that case, they have likely trained you to register their contempt, hostility, frustration, and disapproval, all while putting on a pleasant public persona. In other words, they can look charming and charismatic to others while sending you a different message. Here's a list of some of the possibilities:

- staring
- gritting teeth
- winking
- eyes half-mast
- clenching jaw
- sneer (lip pulled up on one side)
- pursed lips
- growling
- biting lip
- flared nostrils
- bulging temples
- heavy exhale
- loud inhale
- no eye contact
- turning the body away
- moving closer or away suddenly

The list is limitless and personal to the manipulator. They are continually looking for and refining non-verbal behaviors and trying them out on you to see how you react. It's essential that you actively watch for these clues in order to identify that manipulation is taking place.

Scan the code above with your smartphone camera to watch a short video explanation **Non-Verbal Communication** Outwitting Techniques.

Each of these self-protection techniques may sound similar. Once you can identify whether your manipulator is receptive to Ethos, Pathos, or Logos, you will notice that each of these techniques contains words and tone designed to fit the particular mode of communication that works best to get your manipulator to respond. When they recognize that you have become aware of the tactic they are using, they will quickly abandon it.

Become familiar with the description of the tactics that a manipulator will use so that you can subconsciously identify the tactic and start to connect the dots with past conversations or behaviors. When you can do that, you will recognize when they occur in real-time and realize they are not isolated or random. Manipulators calculate the use of these tactics. Of course, they may vary the wording or particular references to keep you unaware. The same is true for your responses to these tactics. The words we are suggesting here are not the only things you can say. They will give you the general attitude and demeanor that you want to show. When we suggest how to say them, such as volume, speed, facial expression, or body language, we urge that you not vary from that too much. Your manipulator will tune in to your words, of course, but they are just as interested in the manner in which you present yourself. So, do your best to capture the directions we gave you on how to say the words for each technique.

The main objective of the self-protection technique is to put the manipulator on notice that you know what is happening. That awareness makes you unattractive as a target. It's also important for you to be mindful that when the manipulator gets agitated, mean, or impatient - you are succeeding! Always remember that this is what success looks like, and don't get apathetic about paying attention. Again, if you believe you may be in physical danger, say whatever you need to say to get away safely. Remember, mark it in your notes when you suspect that one of these tactics is being used!

7

Self Protection Skills
You Will Need

IN THE PREVIOUS chapter, you learned the techniques to use in real-time, as the manipulation is happening. Those words and directions for delivery give you specific defenses you will need on the spot.

Skills are the more general abilities you must have to be adept at handling any situation. Skills are often those things we do with little or no thought, learned at another time or age, and are now in our subconscious mind. When needed, we just call on them, and they appear. Handling a fork, walking, and buttoning a shirt are all examples of the type of skills that most people have acquired and have unconscious competence in executing. While you are learning new skills, you are in the stage of conscious incompetence, which requires much more energy and focus. Over time you will become adept and move toward unconscious competence when skills become automatic or habitual. There are additional skills you will need in addition to the communication techniques:

Control Accessibility - Control your availability, whether on the phone, computer, or in person. Avoid responding immediately to the manipulator, which is an easy and subtle way to train them that YOU will decide when to respond. Develop the mindset that it is appropriate and helpful to change your accessibility. This can be difficult if you work or live with them. Do your best to find ways to prevent contact, communication, or being in the presence of your manipulator.

EXERCISE 1:

Limit and control the access others have to you by committing to do the items below:

TO - DO	DONE?
Make all social media accounts private	
Go through contacts on social media and eliminate those you do not recognize	
Don't answer calls from unknown numbers	
Change your voicemail message so that you don't identify yourself	
Google yourself and try to remove any personal information that is public	
Don't allow others to tag you in social media without your approval first	
Never answer your door unless you know who is on the other side	
Stay alert to who is around you when in public so you aren't caught off guard	

Build Confidence - As you become practiced and proficient at outwitting the manipulator, your confidence will grow, and the probability of being a target will diminish. At the beginning of developing self-protection techniques, it will take self-discipline and attention to details that may seem small or insignificant. One of the main targets of your manipulator is your self-confidence. If they can cause you to question your talents, your role in the family, the organization, or even your sanity, they will be much more able to manipulate you. You must make a conscious decision to bolster your mindset.

Think about yourself as a valuable and viable human being, a person worthy of respect. Consider the skills and contributions you make to others. Remember the things you are inherently good at as well as those that are studied and earned. Think about the times and people with whom you have had fun and pleasure. There are friends you like spending time with who also like spending time with you, and you can make a list of reasons why this is true. These are the kind of thoughts and beliefs that make up your mindset. They are the thoughts that your manipulator wants to prevent you from forming. They exploit ideas and opinions to tell a false story. Don't allow it!

You are the owner and creator of your own thoughts and beliefs. You shape your confidence and behavior. Don't allow a manipulator to take that away from you. You deserve to set and protect your thoughts and mindset.

EXERCISE 2:

Write specific things you can do to build your confidence:

_____

_____

_____

_____

_____

List all of the things you are good at doing:

_____

_____

_____

_____

_____

List the things you would like to strengthen in yourself:

_____

_____

_____

_____

_____

List one specific action you can take to strengthen each thing you listed above. Give yourself a deadline to execute it.

_____

_____

_____

_____

_____

Control Your Emotions - Remember, the goal of manipulating or controlling the momentum of the moment is to trigger your emotions. Managing your reactions requires a lot of practice. This doesn't mean that you must hide or deny your emotions. The keyword is "manage." It means being aware of what triggers or ignites an emotional reaction in you to prepare in advance. Then, protecting yourself when your manipulator tries to use your emotions against you. You must learn to identify the tricks that they use to trigger you. Don't deny your right to have emotions, just learn to control them when dealing with your manipulator.

EXERCISE 3:

Managing your emotions is one of the HARDEST things to do! Don't deny your right to have emotions, just learn to control them when dealing with your manipulator. Practice respond-ing instead of reacting. Do you know the difference? Reacting is immediate and emotional. You give the manipulator exactly what they want, which is control over your emotions. Responding is thoughtful. Take a pause, think about it, or postpone your response. Make a conscious choice about how you will react.

Making a plan:

The next time _____ says _____. I will respond in the following way:

_____

_____

_____

_____

_____

Control Your Non-Verbal Behavior - It is often easier to control what you say than it is to control what you do. We mean the ability to unknowingly communicate to the manipulator by using subtle non-verbal facial expressions and movement. This could mean an eye movement, a smile or frown, head movement, or other bodily gestures. These kinds of behaviors, which are normal in most conversations, are information to a manipulator who is watching them for insight into your vulnerability.

This may seem extreme to you; however, manipulators watch closely for non-verbal cues that you give them. It may take a bit of effort on your part to recognize and be aware that you are giving these signals; however, the effort will be worth it. Controlling these will have the added benefit of strengthening your self-confidence.

A final note on non-verbal behaviors: many manipulators will become aware of your new sense of control and decide that you are a more difficult target and move on to someone else. That's a good thing!

EXERCISE 4:

Look in a mirror while you are on the phone and practice controlling your facial expressions. This will also help you become more aware of how it feels to make certain expressions and to envision what it looks like, and control it when necessary.

Control Tone, Volume, Speed, and Inflection - Each of these individual parts of your speech shapes the impression you give. As we have been saying throughout the book, it is to your benefit to control as much as you can when you are in the presence of your manipulator. These parts of speaking are totally in your control.

Normally, you don't think much about these things or need to make an effort. When you are dealing with a manipulator, that all changes. Each exchange you have with your manipulator will require your attention to individual speaking elements because each one: tone, volume, speed, and inflection, reveal specific information. Don't forget that you are a target, and the goal is to control.

You can protect yourself by being aware and intentional when considering aspects of your speech. In the previous chapter, we gave you some specific directions for using words, audio, and visual clues in our examples. Those suggestions are carefully designed for each of the particular tactics with which you are dealing. Here, we'd like to share some ways to build your mind-set about speaking, and suggest that you think about being flat or more monotone so that the manipulator is challenged to discern which things are your triggers.

As you practice using these techniques from the last chapter out loud, also practice controlling each small speaking element. This is going to be difficult because you may have strong emotional reactions to what is happening. Try your best to not allow your emotions to be accidentally revealed. Controlling each aspect of your speech is a definite way to build your confidence and solidify your strength against what is being said to or about you.

EXERCISE 5:

Practice saying things that you might say in response to a manipulative tactic and consider the following:

- Use a flat, monotone sound.

- Open a voice recorder app on your phone. Listen back and assess whether you are controlling how you feel with your delivery style.

- Practice multiple times until you are proficient speaking with a flat, monotone delivery. That type of speech pattern will prevent the manipulator from getting more information to exploit you.

Create a Mindset of Irrelevance and Detachment - By doing this, you will be able to control your reactions better, both verbally and non-verbally. Communication begins with your mindset, so first engage the brain before putting the mouth in action! It can be challenging to do because living with a manipulator seldom allows YOU or YOUR interests any time, space, or importance.

Your manipulator will not let you think. They may profess to give you space, but it will always be on their terms, and telling you that is only another tactic of manipulation. You must develop a mindset of irrelevance and detachment for yourself. That means that once you have clearly identified that you are a target of manipulation, you must make a conscious plan to make decisions that help retain your self-worth, confidence, sense of wellbeing, and independence. This is mostly a mindset matter. Believe in your ability to avoid being emotionally triggered or overly reactive to the tactics being used.

You may not be able to distance yourself from your manipulator physically, but you can decide to stay in control of your reactions. This will be difficult, and we know it will take time. As they recognize that you are in control, they will retreat and look for a more vulnerable target.

EXERCISE 6:

How do you create a mindset of irrelevance? You need to be more responsive and less reactive with a manipulator. This will give you more control over your emotions and the momentum of the moment. You have to create Martial Law in your brain, which is zero tolerance for thinking about the manipulator's thoughts, feelings, actions, inactions, reactions, intentions, inconsistencies, promises, possibilities, and potential. ALL of it must become insignificant. The only way for you to take back your power is to set the intention that you will not allow someone else to dictate your life. Every time you start thinking about the tactics used by your manipulator to devalue your self-worth, say, "STOP!" aloud.

If possible, walk to a mirror and look into your own eyes and say, "STOP!" Then, you must direct your brain to think about something else.

We have created a list called P.A.D. - Positive Actions for Distraction. The criteria for P.A.D. is any activity that moves you forward. It can be self-care, organizing, cleaning, or something joyful and fun. We broke this list down into time segments of 15 minutes, 1-2 hours, half-day activities, and full-day activities. This is SO helpful to have handy when you find yourself spiraling with negative thoughts. It can easily happen when you have some time on your hands. Prepare a list of activities, pick something off the menu, and throw yourself into it. This is a powerful exercise and starts changing your life for the better immediately. Here is a sample list:

Positive Actions for Distraction P.A.D.			
15 minute activities	**1-2 hour activities**	**1/2 day activities**	**Full-day activities**
Dance to your favorite songs	Call cell phone and/or cable and make sure you have the best plan	Organize a closet, basement, or garage	Ask a friend to go on a day hike and pack a picnic
Organize your Tupperware drawer	Post three unused items for sale on the internet	Do yoga, meditation and take an Epsom salt bath	Indulge in your hobby, and if you don't have one, start!
Write a note of gratitude to someone and mail it	Go through your digital photos and delete the bad ones	Rake leaves, shovel snow plant some flowers, weed the yard	Paint a room in your house and move the furniture around
Glue something that's broken	Eliminate people from your social media accounts	Drive to a new town and explore it as if you were a travel reviewer	Spend the day baking or cooking delicious things to share with others

Positive Actions for Distraction P.A.D.			
15 minute activities	**1-2 hour activities**	**1/2 day activities**	**Full-day activities**
Scrub the kitchen floor while listening to a podcast	Create a budget by analyzing your past expenses	Research places to volunteer and reach out to them	Go on Youtube and learn to do something new like belly dancing, embroidery, using a drill, polishing pots and pans

Make Your Own P.A.D.:

Positive Actions for Distraction P.A.D.			

Embrace the Definition of Healthy Relationships - Healthy relationships are based on trust and communication. To help you assess whether or not you are in a healthy relationship, here are three essential questions you should be able to ask and receive an affirmative response:

- Are you able to identify how you feel at the moment? You may have multiple and/or conflicting emotions.

- Are you able to describe your emotions/feelings verbally using "I" statements?

- Does the other person show respect for your feelings and, most importantly, demonstrate their respect by changing their behavior?

If you find that you are stuck repeating steps one and two, and step three either never happens or happens temporarily, you are in an unhealthy and/or manipulative relationship!

Do you know who your allies are? You must know how to identify them. They require 3 things:

1. You know them well

2. They know you well

3. They want to see you succeed, they celebrate it, they are not envious or jealous

Knowing yourself, how you feel, and assessing allies and healthy relationships are essential to your happiness.

EXERCISE 7:

1. Are you able to identify how you feel in the moment? Write about the last time you were emotional, what you were feeling, and why. You may have multiple and/or conflicting emotions. Note each of them here:

_____

_____

_____

_____

_____

_____

2. Are you able to describe your emotions/feelings verbally using "I" statements? Try to do it now using the example in step 1 and write it here:

_____

_____

_____

_____

_____

_____

3. Does the other person in your personal or professional relationship show respect for your feelings and most importantly demonstrate their respect by changing their behavior when you share the above statements with them? YES or NO

_____

_____

_____

_____

Think of a time where you did steps 1 and 2 above with someone. Did they take your feelings to heart by changing the behavior you found hurtful? Do you have a relationship with someone where you can expect that your feelings are respected, accepted and they demonstrate it by not repeating the hurtful behavior?

Who is that person?

_____

4. Who are the people who have demonstrated that they don't care about your feelings? List them here:

_____

_____

_____

_____

_____

Develop Feistiness - Develop this if you don't have it! Let's be clear that we are not suggesting that you become a nasty or aggressive person. The kind of "feistiness" we are talking about is more of a mindset to have when in the presence of your manipulator. This mindset will help you protect yourself by giving the manipulator a signal that says that you will not be pressured, bullied, intimidated, or in any other way, be pushed into some negative feeling or action. This is your ability to channel your energy into persistent, unwavering self-protection rather than feeling embarrassed, weak, or filled with self-doubt.

Feistiness does not mean being cruel or nasty, or insulting, as that would erode your confidence. Feistiness can be indicated by responding quickly to comments or behaviors that are rude, crude, or disturbing. It also means speaking a little faster than normal, increasing your volume slightly, facing your manipulator more directly if possible. Use shorter rather than longer statements.

All of this may be alien to your normal communication style. However, let's remember who and what you are dealing with – the manipulator exploits typical communication. You will need to move out of your comfort zone to send the message that you are strong. Finally, it is a good idea actually to practice new techniques of communication out loud. It may feel strange, but it is a good way to get more comfortable with feistiness as a self-protection techni

EXERCISE 8:

This can be a tough skill to develop. Almost everyone has a situation in which even the shyest people-pleaser will speak up. Can you remember a time in which you spoke up to the power figure or establishment regarding an injustice? Describe the situation here:

_____

_____

_____

_____

_____

_____

Where did you feel it the most in your body: tight chest? queasy stomach? shaky legs? quivering voice? headache?

_____

_____

_____

_____

_____

_____

This is normal, and it's helpful for you to know how it manifests in you physically when you speak up and/or confront someone. It's good to know, and even better to accept that this is a normal occurrence. Almost everyone feels anxious and nervous when they speak up for themselves.

The best thing that will help you stay in control is diaphragmatic breathing. The diaphragm is a muscle and can be trained like any other muscle. It is the normal and most healthy way to breathe. It distributes oxygen that you take in by inhaling and directs it to the brain through oxygenation. This allows you to control your physical and emotional reactions better.

To test if you are breathing diaphragmatically, put one hand on your belly (actually, it's your diaphragm) and the other hand on your upper chest. When you breathe in, you should feel your belly move *out*. When you breathe out, you should feel your belly move *in*. You should feel little or no motion in your upper chest. If you do not feel these correct motions, try again until you can control this properly. It may take a bit of repeating to get it. When you can breathe this way, it will relax your entire body.

The best way to practice and strengthen this diaphragm muscle (yes, it is a muscle) is to count from 1 to 20 as you are exhaling. At first, your count may not be long, but as you practice, it will get stronger, and you will be able to reach 20. You will also feel the relaxation of your body and reduce the thoughts that produce anxiety.

Identify Triggers and Deactivate - This is one of the most important self-protection skills to practice. If you don't identify what triggers you, your manipulator will. This is a manipulator superpower. Knowing what upsets you, what annoys you, what makes you feel uncomfortable, etc., is a strong step in the right direction of not being a target of manipulation. Most people do know some of the things that trigger an automatic emotional response for them. What we are suggesting is that you go a bit further and spend time investigating your deeply held beliefs, the values that direct your life, and the way you interact with others.

Be brutally honest with yourself. You don't have to reveal any of your thoughts or discoveries to anyone else. When you can do this, you will have a much greater understanding of what we have been referring to as your mindset. The ability to identify your triggers will help apply the techniques we identified in Chapter 6.

EXERCISE 9:

Your emotional hooks are those things that trigger you. They disrupt any feeling of calm or comfort. When your manipulator knows what your hooks are, they will use them regularly. It is worth your time and effort to honestly evaluate what hooks you. These could be things that you might not be overtly aware of and can be related to any number of items, topics, words, facial expressions, tone of voice, and more that, for whatever reason, stir a negative feeling in you. Assume that your manipulator also knows what those things are and will use them as a tactic to control your emotions and behaviors at the moment. Listen for keywords, sounds, or expressions that they use to trigger you, and note them in the following boxes.

My Emotional Hooks
Example: I get very irritated when someone interrupts me when I'm telling a story.

When you can listen for and link these words, sounds, and expressions to the tactic being used, you will learn how to protect yourself when you hear them in the future. It is valuable to know what those hooks are for you. At this point, it is not important for you to know why these things hook you. This is a private list, so don't be shy about identifying them here. Nothing is too small or insignificant if it stirs a negative or uncomfortable feeling in you.

Inquiring Mind - Remember these words from a television commercial? -"*Inquiring minds want to know*!" This is a great mindset to have as you will be sure to ask questions all the time. Who? What? Where? When? Why? (The 5 Ws). The person asking the questions is in control of the *momentum of the moment*. Most manipulators have spent time using these 5 Ws to plan strategies and tactics for a particular situation. You will be better prepared to counter the tactics when you have thought through The 5 Ws and their possible use.

Prepare yourself by dedicating time and effort to building your self-protection techniques when you are not in the presence of your manipulator. Rather than allowing yourself to be triggered in the moment, you can try asking one or more questions. You will probably find that your manipulator will evade answering, try changing the subject, or ask you why you ask the questions. You don't need to go into a lot of explanation. Simply reply with something simple like, "*Just curious, but ...*" or " *Your comments started me thinking.*" This is also a fast way to expose inconsistencies and outright lies.

Practice Note-taking - To uncover the manipulator, you will need to watch for patterns and be aware of the context. We're not trying to create paranoia; however, the sooner you can identify a manipulator, the sooner you can get away. You can reduce the collateral damage to your psyche, bank account, life, and the torrent of little things that happen. Your brain won't be able to keep up with each incident. Thoroughly documenting the events will reveal the manipulative pattern. Trust your judgment and instinct. Even though a word, gesture, look, or comment may seem tiny or inconsequential, it doesn't mean it is insignificant.

You can create your own notebook, download the OUTWIT app, or use the note pages at the end of this book to keep your journal. The notes will mount up. If you live with a manipulator, they will likely go through all of your personal things. So, it's best if your notes are a bit cryptic; the Outwit app can be more convenient and private.

Make your notebook easy to use and convenient to read later. Here is an example of how to organize the content:

DATE	EVENT	CONTEXT	TACTIC
4/2/20	out to dinner with Bob and Sue	there couple was talking and joking about past relationships	Non-verbal disapproval, he became silent, gritted teeth, and embarrassed me

Remember You Have Free Will - the manipulator's goal is to get you to forget that you have Free Will, the power of acting without the constraint of necessity or fate; the ability to act at one's own discretion. You ALWAYS, no matter what, have a CHOICE. Remember to exercise your Free Will in the moment. Tattoo it on your mind and heart! Keep this skill at the ready and use it when needed. Free Will is a major part of the mindset that allows you to maintain control. The more strongly you integrate this belief, the more comfortable you will be with practicing the techniques identified here.

EXERCISE 10:

Many of us find ourselves in situations where we feel we have "no choice" or obligated to say or behave in a specific way, and we forget we don't have to! Here are some things you can do to exercise and strengthen your free will. After each exercise, make a note of your internal feelings and thoughts.

1. Next time you get an invitation to something, even if you want to accept it, respond with "*I'll take it into consideration and let you know.*" Give no excuse or explanation, just a polite smile. You will be taking control of the interaction. That will feel good.

    _____

    _____

    _____

    _____

    _____

2. In the next planning discussion, whether at work or family vacations/holidays, add your thoughts/opinions to the discussion with a confident delivery. Do not defend your position. Have the mindset that your opinion/insight is valuable, you have the right to share it, and that your contribution will be valued.

    _____

    _____

    _____

    _____

    _____

3. Break your patterns! Don't sit in the same chair or say the same thing you always do. Think about it strategically and intentionally instead.

_____

_____

_____

_____

_____

4. Is there someone you are always expected to respond to immediately? Do something for yourself that is fun and/or self-care oriented and put your phone on "Do Not Disturb"; make this a habit. If someone is upset because you didn't respond, don't give an explanation or apology. Say the following instead: "*There are times when I need to focus without interruption, and when that is the case, I will be unreachable for a period of time.*" PERIOD, no more words.

Your time is your own, and you have a right to set those boundaries. This will be more difficult if you are at work. Don't do anything that would jeopardize your work security. You will need to be more selective in identifying times and people who deserve this treatment in each setting. Still, it will be your choice. Make a list of times that you can take this action.

_____

_____

_____

_____

_____

Show Intolerance for Manipulative Communication - There is an enormous cost to allowing or tolerating manipulation. What you may not realize is that your tolerance (meaning you don't speak up in the moment) helps to grow the contempt your manipulator has for you. They think of you as weak, stupid, and gullible when they get away with applying the tactics listed in this book. It will NEVER get better, only worse.

Targets will often rationalize the manipulator's behavior or feel like the moment wasn't appropriate to speak up. Naturally, you will have to make that judgment each time. We're not suggesting that you must become combative in every situation and certainly not submissive. We do want you to feel empowered to defend yourself. Sometimes this intolerance we are talking about must be practiced internally. Even if you find it is not productive to actually respond in the moment, in your mind, make that conscious decision. Be in charge of your thoughts, as well as your behaviors.

You will find it comforting and empowering to know that you recognized the manipulative tactic and made a strategic decision as to how to respond. This is the equivalent of you controlling the momentum of the moment. If you allow the tactics to take place and do not react outwardly, your manipulator's dislike for you will grow. Even if they are love bombing you, they still are holding you in contempt simultaneously.

The sounds and behavior of love bombing can seem comforting. Don't be fooled! Be patient with yourself. Sometimes it takes years, decades, or even half a century (as in Robin's case!) to figure it out. Practice your skills of observation. Whenever anything seems out of place or questionable, remember to mark it in your notes. It is important to develop the self-protection skill of intolerance for manipulative communication.

EXERCISE 11:

What are you tolerating? Take a moment to sit quietly and think about what you *do not want* to tolerate. Use the sample questions below to prompt your thinking and then allow yourself to freely write your non-negotiables.

QUESTIONS	YES/NO	CONSEQUENCES (be specific)
Will you tolerate someone lying to you? **If not, determine the consequence.**		
Will you tolerate someone making disparaging comments toward you? **If not, determine the consequence.**		
Will you tolerate someone interrupting you when you are speaking? **If not, determine the consequence.**		
Will you tolerate someone appropriating your ideas, jokes, insights and presenting them as their own? **If not, determine the consequence.**		

QUESTIONS	YES/NO	CONSEQUENCES (be specific)
Will you tolerate someone representing your perspectives, emotions, opinions? Speaking for you? **If not, determine the consequence.**		
Will you tolerate someone obligating you to do something for someone else? **If not, determine the consequence.**		
Will you tolerate someone expecting you to respond to them immediately for a non-emergency? **If not, determine the consequence.**		

Use Active Listening - This is NOT like passive hearing. You are listening for intent, nuance, tone, expressions, especially watching where their eyes travel on each word. This important skill can be developed and strengthened. Being an active listener means being able to pay attention to what is happening and being said. It is also important to go beyond paying attention. You must learn to focus on the words and delivery methods of the manipulator. Attention is the overall ability to be aware of all the sounds around you. Focus is the specific ability to give all your attention to the specific behaviors of the manipulator.

Manipulators rely on you not being able to focus. Their expectation may well be that you are paying attention but not able to actually focus because the kids need you, or you are on the phone, or you are in a hurry to go someplace, and you are not able to notice subtle clues about what they do or say. They are using some elements of the context surrounding you to use a manipulative tactic to control the momentum of the moment. If you can pay attention AND focus, you will be better equipped to defend yourself. The devil is in the details. If a comment, gesture, facial expression, anything seems odd, don't dismiss it as your imagination; mark it in your notes.

Listening can be either active or passive. The difference is simple. Passive listening is hearing the sounds and not giving any overt indications of engagement. Active listening gives specific attention or focus to what you're hearing. You acknowledge what is being said using paralanguage or short expressions such as, *"oh,"* *"I see,"* *"really,"* or *"no kidding."* Head nodding and facial expressions are other examples of paralanguage. Active listening is a skill worth practicing and learning for use in identifying the tactics used by your manipulator.

6 Things You Can do to Strengthen Your Skill of Active Listening:

1. **Get Ready to Listen.** You will want to be in a location or situation where you will not be distracted as much as possible.

2. **Pay Attention.** You have the ability to be generally aware of the sounds around you. As you read these words, for example, there may be several sounds and noises within your hearing distance. Normally, you will be aware of them but not giving them much attention. If you focus, you make a conscious choice to give your full attention to a specific thing within your attention span. Focusing is a key skill of active listening that will help you isolate and address specific tactics being used. Focus is also a critical listening skill because your manipulator often conflates tactics to confuse you.

3. **Control your Biases.** This may be one of the most difficult skills you ever have to learn. Let's be clear that we are not saying that you should not have biases. We all have biases. We have them about almost everything. Some people like chocolate more than vanilla. Some people like reading a book more than playing a sport. We could go on and on. We all have biases about almost everything. That is not a bad thing. The key is having "control" over showing them.

   You surely have biases and strong feelings about the manipulator in your life. These biases are real and deserved. We urge you to learn how to control those thoughts and behaviors that expose your bias when you are in that person's presence. If they can detect your preferences, they will use them to exploit you. Controlling your biases will prevent the manipulator from having more ammunition against you.

4. **Probe for Information.** If you do not clearly understand something, ask questions of clarification. As you learned in the book, several manipulation tactics work best when

you are not listening carefully. Manipulators make constant efforts to obfuscate and confuse you with twisted logic and emotional language. The simple act of asking clarifying questions will send a message to the manipulator that you control the interaction and are not intimidated into simply accepting what is said.

5. **Use Paraphrasing.** Show that you can focus and not be confused. Paraphrasing means that you repeat what was just said in your own words. You don't have to be exact with the words you choose. If the paraphrasing is incorrect, that will probably give the manipulator an opening to criticize or make fun of you. Expect it. Then, ask for clarification of what was missed. Paraphrase again until you get it right. Your persistence will show self-determination for knowledge. Don't be deterred by the snide or snarky remarks that manipulators use to intimidate you. Your "stick-to-it-tive-ness" will send a strong signal that you are not giving up the momentum of the moment.

6. **Use Paralanguage.** This may be a strange word for you. We briefly touched on paralanguage in the topic of active listening referring to short sounds that you use to show that you are paying focused attention. They include vocalized sounds like *"um," "oh," "er," "hmph,"* and other short expressions like, *"wow," "really,"* and *"no way."* You may have a few favorites of your own. Paralanguage also includes nodding your head, raising your eyebrows, squinting, and other small body language movements. Be careful not to send the wrong or unintended message by using paralanguage when you are not aware of it. Identify your paralanguage habits and learn to control it.

EXERCISE 12:

Ask a friend to practice listening with you by allowing you to stop the conversation and paraphrase what you just heard.

Manipulators often use the same tactics over and over. Make it a point to focus and identify the tactic that was just used. If you feel safe in the moment, you can call out manipulator. Check or verify the tactics by going over the complete list in Chapter 6.

If possible, record (check your state laws on recording) a conversation with your manipulator. Later, play it back and see if you can identify the tactics used during the conversation. Again, see the complete list of tactics in Chapter 6.

As you listen to another person speaking, try to identify (to yourself, of course) whether that person is using Ethos, Pathos, or Logos language as they speak.

Visualize a Protective Energy Field - this may sound too "woo woo" to you but do it anyway! What do you have to lose? Many people have found this to be very helpful. Imagination and intention are powerful tools. It's been scientifically proven that humans are surrounded by an electromagnetic field (see resource section). It's also widely accepted that we create reality and affect our cells (health) based on how we think.

Whether you accept this or not, you have nothing to lose by visualizing a protective bubble surrounding you each time you engage your manipulator. It takes 10 seconds or less of thought time. If you feel icky after an encounter, imagine a shower of white light clearing your energy field. You have nothing to lose and everything to gain by investing 10 seconds in this process.

EXERCISE 13:

Before you engage with your manipulator, listen to our recording on the Outwit App to prepare yourself or visualize the following:

Imagine yourself at the center of a beautiful iridescent bubble. This bubble extends three feet out of your body in all directions. The bubble acts as a loving boundary and filter, keeping you healthy and whole inside. Nothing can permeate this bubble that is harmful or upsetting to you. You can see those energy barbs being launched, but they just bounce off the bubble and fall away into space.

Can you see yourself inside the bubble? You have a huge smile on your face. You know and accept that you are ONLY responsible for your own thoughts, words, actions, and feelings. Everything outside your bubble is not your responsibility, and you don't have to worry about it. Your only job is to take care of yourself and let life take care of everyone else. Whenever you feel negative energy, invoke the bubble in your mind's eye.

You don't have to believe in this for it to work, do it anyway. You have nothing to lose. When it comes to dealing with a manipulator, you will need ALL the help you can get.

8
Outwit Table

THIS CHAPTER'S **OUTWIT Table** will help you quickly reference the 24 most commonly used manipulation tactics you learned in Chapter 6. On the left side is the tactic used by the manipulator, and on the right side, you will see a description of the technique for dealing with that particular manipulative tactic. It is important that you take the time to practice these techniques and put them in your own words or use the wording we have suggested in Chapter 6.

Remember, your manipulator has only one strategy - to control you by controlling the *momentum of the moment.* So, remaining calm during the flood of the tactics will, in itself, be great self-protection. Overt displays of emotion will be regarded as a WIN by the manipulator. In the beginning, strive for recognition of the tactic being used. In time, your level of awareness and skill in utilizing the techniques will increase. The good news is that as your skill improves in using these techniques, your manipulator may well move on to a more vulnerable target.

Summary of Manipulator Tactics and Target's Techniques	
Manipulator's Tactic	**Technique to Outwit**
Ambiguity Purposely structuring words/ sentences to have multiple meanings or interpretations	Be persistent about clarifying questions. Play dumb about implications.
Apophysis a rhetorical comment where the manipulator brings up a subject by either denying it or denying that it should be brought up.	Use humor. "*HAHA I get it. You are saying that you won't talk about something, BY talking about it. That's funny.*" Or appeal to the ever-present ego by saying something like, "*How clever of you to put it like that.*"
Bullying Verbal personal attacks that intimidate. Also non-verbal behavior and/or physical posturing with aggressive energy causing a feeling of fear or insecurity.	Cease communication immediately. Hang up, leave the building, and if you can't don't respond.
Blame To hold responsible; find fault with, place the responsibility for something on someone else, or censure.	Broken record technique can be effective here. You simply keep repeating - "*I'm not the one to blame here.*" or "*I refuse to accept any blame.*"

Summary of Manipulator Tactics and Target's Techniques	
Manipulator's Tactic	**Technique to Outwit**
Calculation and Planning Events Events that are the result of calculation and planning but are perceived by the target/mark to be a coincidence.	In these situations, ask questions. Ask a lot of questions for clarification and justification, and be persistent.
Changing the Subject The manipulator pivots to a different subject, usually one that's more attractive to the target.	In a calm, non-accusatory voice you can say, "*I notice that you are changing the subject. Is there a reason for that?*" Or, with a stronger voice, ask, "*Why are you changing the subject?*"
Conflation Mixing two distinct thoughts/events as if they were one.	It is often helpful to ignore the conflation and continue to focus only on the original subject, or point out the conflation and insist on addressing each thing separately.
Creating Self Doubt This method is used by a manipulator in an insidious way often through non-verbal disapproval or verbally packaged as a "joke."	State your opinions declaratively with volume and in a confident tone, ignore their implications to create self-doubt.

Summary of Manipulator Tactics and Target's Techniques	
Manipulator's Tactic	**Technique to Outwit**
Dictating feelings Interpreting your feelings and telling how you feel	Use humor if you can and correct immediately and consistently.
Gaslighting Denying and/or redefining reality - insisting that something isn't true or didn't happen even though you may have witnessed it first-hand.	Remain calm and state your reality/perception of events in a confident tone with direct eye contact. Agree to disagree, this notifies the manipulator that you are not accepting their narrative.
Grooming (Love bombing) Kindness, romance, flattery, adoration, devotion, fairytale, and fun activities all with a hidden agenda to gain control over the target.	It's important that no matter how good the compliments feel, you receive them neutrally, and avoid fawning.
Hurt and Rescue Creating a calculated crisis often used to incite emotions in the target so that the manipulator can then be the hero and rescue the target or solve the problem/crisis.	Avoid receiving the help, solution, or answer from the manipulator who caused the problem.

Summary of Manipulator Tactics and Target's Techniques	
Manipulator's Tactic	**Technique to Outwit**
Invalidation Minimizing your opinions, feelings, and perceptions, demonstrating disregard for you non-verbally and verbally. See "Creating Self Doubt" above.	It's best to make an "I" statement, short and strong to put the manipulator on notice that you see what's happening. *"I won't continue this conversation without you acknowledging my feelings."* Then FOLLOW THROUGH!
Irony Meaning anything except the literal meaning of the word, often used as humor, but intended to embarrass.	Don't show embarrassment. Ignore the irony and respond to the words literally, at face value.
Leveraging Others Using a third party to join in overtly or covertly. *"Everyone thinks your nuts"* or *"your brother agrees that no-one in the family likes you."*	Ignore the statements. Remember to control your non-verbal reaction (poker face). You will know you are succeeding when the statements escalate.
Name Calling A comparison to people you despise. *"You're just like your mother"* or just good old-fashioned *"You're such a bitch!"*	*"The next time you call me a name this conversation will end abruptly."* Then DO IT by leaving, hanging up, or stop speaking.

Summary of Manipulator Tactics and Target's Techniques	
Manipulator's Tactic	**Technique to Outwit**
Non-verbal Disapproval and Approval Facial expression and para-language, this is in use constantly with many of the other methods listed here.	Try hard to ignore non-verbal communication. Focus on the face value of the words only, refuse to accept the subtext.
Public Humiliation Threatening to embarrass you in order to control you, using information that will knowingly hurt you, typically gained in confidence about a personal insecurity.	The only way to diffuse it is to REFUSE to feel humiliated no matter what. Avoid disclosing personal information so you don't embolden them.
Reframing a Past Event The manipulator twists and distorts the facts of a past event to benefit their agenda.	The best response is *"Hmm I don't remember it that way at all, well to each his own."* Then change the subject. Saying anything more will play into their hands.
Repetition of False Information Confidently repeating false facts until you accept it.	Your denial or rejection will be used against you and will be seen as an admission by observers. Embrace the false information with humor/sarcasm and make a joke of it by adding your own exaggeration to the narrative.

Summary of Manipulator Tactics and Target's Techniques	
Manipulator's Tactic	**Technique to Outwit**
Sarcasm Words used in distaste often to embarrass others.	Interpret literally or show NO reaction.
Use of a Surrogate Using another person to manipulate.	Recognize that surrogates have been enlisted because the manipulator needs help with their agenda. Ignore the surrogate and/or ask them to stay out of it.
Word Use, Choice, and Inflection Using words and/or their delivery to embarrass.	These statements are designed to make you feel shame. Review the facts and don't internalize this message!
Non Verbal Tactics	Facial expressions and micro-expressions that may only be recognized by your subconscious rather than your conscious mind. Also includes gestures and movements.

9

More on Mindset and Free Will

KNOWING, BUILDING, AND controlling your mindset is critical to everything you do. The things you do and think are consistently made up of your attitudes, beliefs, and values, all of which are housed in your mind. Attitudes become thoughts. Thoughts become words. Words tell the manipulator a lot about how to approach you.

Few people ever take the time to evaluate their mindset and why they believe certain thoughts and ideas. Manipulators do. If they can assess what is in your mindset, they will find ways to manipulate you. That is why you need to become familiar with the attitudes, beliefs, and values you hold. We are not suggesting that there is a right or wrong here. We do not want you to think we are telling you what should be in your mindset. Nor are we suggesting it's your fault if you are manipulated. However, we are letting you know that your attitudes, beliefs, and values will make you more or less of a target to manipulators. For instance, if you believe that you are not worthy of respect, love, or common good treatment, your behavior may lead to becoming a prime target for manipulation. If you place a low value on your level of intelligence or education, your speech and other behaviors will communicate a weakness as well. Manipulators will surely exploit that aspect of your mindset. You must investigate and evaluate your thoughts as you learn how to protect yourself from manipulators. Give yourself the gift of investigating:

- *why you believe the things you do*

- *why you act and react to things the way you do*

- *why you like or dislike some things*

You will be forced to take a deep and quiet look into the attitudes you have about all those things. How did you get those thoughts or feelings? Who influenced you as you grew into adulthood? What role did family or teachers have in shaping your beliefs? These questions and their answers will help you understand why mindset is important as you learn how to protect yourself from manipulators.

One important aspect of mindset we want to impress on you pertains to free will. The main goal of the manipulator is to make you forget that you ALWAYS have a choice. Your innate right as a human being is access to free will. You always get to decide who, what, when, why, and how to think your thoughts.

Manipulators dedicate their efforts to making you feel as though you are not worthy of free will. All of their manipulative efforts are implemented to control you. For instance, if you were totally deflated like a balloon on the floor, you are useless to them and would make them look bad for being with you. If you are confident and secure, filled with the agency of free will, you would be floating near the ceiling where they couldn't reach you, and you can go where you like easily (especially if you've cut the string).

The manipulator needs you to be like the balloon 3 days after the party, heavy, slow-moving, and right where they can control you easily. That is why they will use a combination of compliments/praise and insults/criticism through their insidious, sneaky, and underhanded ways centered on controlling each consecutive *momentum of the moment.* As you learned in the preceding chapters, they intend to take away any internal strength, pride, or independence. If you have a strong mindset filled with self-confidence, courage, and self-protection skills and techniques learned in this book, they won't be able to control you.

One of the most consistent tools of leverage for the manipulator is fear, specifically, the fear of public humiliation. They always say people fear public speaking more than death, but we think they got it wrong. It's not fear of public speaking, it's fear of public humiliation, and it's sidekick - embarrassment that may result.

Here's a radical thought for you: Embarrassment is a CHOICE. It certainly may not feel like a choice when your manipulator is acting against you, but it's true. That is a new belief for you to integrate into your mindset. Refusing to feel embarrassed and making that a strong part of your mindset is not only liberating; it's also a wonderful way to model for others how to accept human frailties. A strong mindset is constructed by your conscious decisions and the attitudes, beliefs, and values you choose in life.

Let's first establish what we mean by "Mind." There is a common misnomer that the brain and the mind are the same. They are not. The brain is a physical place within the body and is associated with consciousness. It can be seen, weighed, measured, and carefully identified as an organ. The mind is not physical. It cannot be seen or measured. It is where thoughts, attitudes, and beliefs are housed.

It is the home of the mindset that we have been talking about in this book. Exercising it will take some concentration and focus on your part. The mind affects every part of the body. Controlling your mind will allow you to control the outward expression of emotion that often gives the manipulator information to use against you.

Do the following:

1. **Exercise**. A regular exercise routine will help decrease stress and promote a better mood, enhancing sleep. Start slowly if needed. Try brisk walking at first for about 10 minutes per day. Slowly increase the time until you can conduct a brisk walk for 30 minutes at least three times a week. Even better, add 10 - 20 minutes of aerobic exercise to your daily routine.

2. **Connect.** Find a way to engage in stimulating conversation every day. Be careful not to get hooked on topics that trigger anxiety. Use this as an exchange of ideas rather than a debate or argument.

3. **Find a hobby.** One that requires concentration and focus. Ideally, it will be an enjoyable hobby, that may or may not result in a physical product or a specific outcome. It just needs to take your focus for a period of time, at least every other day.

4. **Practice mindfulness.** To have purposeful thoughts, we must learn controlled focus on a single item or action. Washing your hands is a good example. What does the water feel like? What does the soap feel/smell like? How long are you involved in the act? Eating is an opportunity to practice mindfulness. What does the food taste like? What is the texture of the food? What is the temperature of the food? What teeth are being used to chew the food? These small and private moments of mind control will help to strengthen your mindset. You can choose where, when, and what to focus on in this exercise. Mindfulness is an excellent way to achieve positive and constructive thoughts and keep them under your control.

10

Robin's and Leon's Stories

Robin's Story:

MY MOTHER HAD three children before she was 21, and I was the oldest. She had the fourth when I was 8, handed him to me as a newborn, and showed me how to feed, bathe, and change him. I was in heaven and never played with another fake baby doll again.

Fast forward through many difficult days that turned into years. I came of age at a time when my mother was about to turn 30. She was very jealous of me, my looks, youth, friends ... you name it. I was completely unaware of her jealousy during this time because you just don't think that way about your mom.

Anyone who has been a teenager knows that acceptance by friends and "fitting in" is the highest priority for them. Teenagers can be devastated when ridiculed by the cool kid or by not having the right backpack or sneakers. I could not afford that type of self-absorption. As puberty made me typically more vocal and confrontational about my needs and the inequities in our house, my mother would use embarrassment as her primary tactic to gain control of me. She would:

- tease and mock me in front of my friends
- disparage me in front of her friends

- agree to something important to me and then use it as a weapon
- divulge confidence or vulnerability I shared with her
- lie about everything, frequently reframing events to make herself look good

Often I would react with rage and yell at her. She would then mock me for being *"out of control," "a brat,"* and *"a pain in the ass."* At the time, I had no idea that my mother derived satisfaction from pushing me into a reactive state so that she could accuse me of being the source of her problems. I was born an introspective thinker, creative and curious about people who helped me survive.

My mother once took me to a counselor at age 13 as a punishment. The idea being that the therapist would tell me that she's the boss, and I had to obey her. I resisted going, which made my mother happy. When I came out from the first session smiling and wanting to go back again, she decided to pull the plug on the second appointment.

The therapist had asked to have a moment with me alone. Here's what she said, *"You are not crazy, but your mother is. All you have to do is make it through the next five years, and you can do whatever you want. You will be an adult, and no one can stop you. Don't share this information because I can lose my job."*

I was sad that I wouldn't see her again, but I floated out of there feeling completely empowered with the gift of free will. She was a smart, normal woman, and I looked up to her as the words she spoke that day validated my reality and saved my life. There was an end in sight, and my countdown began. I left home at 17, got a job in Boston, and put myself through college.

The struggles and life experiences that occurred over the next 45 years are the subject of a novel that I will write one day. For this book's purposes, please know that I understand firsthand what it's like to be a target.

Public Humiliation

An epiphany that I had a choice NOT to be embarrassed came to me after one glaring incident when I was 13. I felt I had to do something to change the power my mother held over me.

There was a 7th-grade dance coming up, my first dance, and of course, I wanted to go and talked a lot about it. My best friend Anna and I planned what to wear and talked about whether we would slow dance with a boy. I needed a ride there and bugged my mother repeatedly for a commitment. It was not convenient for her, so she said no. I eventually got her to agree, but she said I would have to leave early, and I'd better be waiting outside for her when she pulled up.

I told my friends I had to leave early, and they didn't understand why. We were having such fun! I was a wreck watching the clock. I knew if I wasn't ready, my mom would come in and embarrass me. I finally said I have to go, and my friend Anna said, "*I'll wait with you.*" What a true friend! We waited and waited, and as was typical for my mom, she was always late and expected everyone to wait for her. Anna said, "*This is ridiculous! Your mom's such a bitch to make you wait when we could be having fun!*" I said, "*You're right. I'm not waiting out here; let's go back in.*"

Ten minutes later, some girls I didn't know were saying my name loudly and looking for me. They told me, "*You have to come right away. Your mom's out there yelling at the principal.*" Yep, there she was, screaming her head off, asking why the cafeteria was so dark, why kids were being allowed to grope each other, and threatening to call all the parents. Naturally, the dance was chaperoned, and no one was behaving the way she described. I just stood there, totally embarrassed as a crowd formed to watch the drama unfold. I thought the embarrassment would kill me. Anna gave me a hug and whispered, "*Your mom is such a bitch!*"

My mom grabbed me, and we got in the car. I told her that I hated her guts and I really hoped she would die soon, and meant it. Then I sat there thinking, who saw her? What would they say? How would this affect my friendships? What would everyone think of me? One advantage was that I was brand new to the school and started mid-year. I went to eight elementary schools and four junior high schools by this point, so I was somewhat unknown. That was Friday. By Monday morning, the school announcements over the loudspeaker in every classroom included the Principal declaring that full lighting would be required at all future dances because of a parent complaint. I was mortified.

I remember making a conscious choice that day that I would detach from my mother's behavior. I would be my own person and disassociate from her. If anybody said anything about the dance, I would tell them - in the words of my 13-year-old vocabulary - that I was embarrassed because my mom was such a bitch. That honesty worked, even with 7th graders! No one blamed me, but more importantly, further introspection helped me realize that my fear of embarrassment gave her power. I decided I would not be embarrassed anymore, no matter what.

It sounds weird, I know, but choosing NOT to feel embarrassed is liberating. What you resist persists. It wasn't the events that were dangerous to me, but the message of control and embarrassment from my mother that I internalized. I have free will and so do you. No one should allow their feelings about an event to define them. Choose instead to accept your humanity in stride, and know that you are never alone in your human frailty. Normal or average humans will empathize with you.

Love-Bombing

I was 24 when I met my now ex-husband, and he was 37. I had moved away from Michigan, where I was the oldest of seven kids and acted as an adult parent my entire life. I was all alone for the first time in my own apartment and feeling very vulnerable; however, I saw myself as strong and confident, capable of handling my situation.

When I met my ex, he love-bombed me ferociously. Having been raised in an environment where my only value was when I was in service to my mother, I found being put on a pedestal of adoration both intoxicating and magical. All of the attention directed to me felt amazing.

Then, moments began cropping up where my ex would display insecurity and jealousy. I would talk about it with my neighbor, Kam, and she told me that he was a "player," and I should leave him. I would see the logic and develop a resolve to end the relationship only to have him change my mind with his charm and love-bombing offensive.

As time went on, I changed my job to work at the same company and moved to his place. Once I was completely moved in, he started showing me the darker side of his deep insecurity. He demanded details of every past relationship and everything I did with other guys. I felt sorry for him and thought I could bolster his confidence with more love and attention. It was hard to reconcile the outward confident, charming man with this private controlling, mean, and scary person. I thought he would mature out of it because he was a smart person. But he never did. Instead, he got worse and worse.

Twenty-two years later, when I finally divorced him, my ex had put our home in foreclosure and attached my name only to half a million dollars in debt. The list of things he did over the course of our marriage was long. However, the point I want to make is not to underestimate the power of love-bombing. Had I had an ally, a therapist, or THIS BOOK, I may have been able to avoid many years of pain. The stories and exercises in this book will help you turn lemons into lemon meringue pie and prevent others from falling prey to a manipulator.

Leon's story:

Leon has three brothers and one sister. They were raised in a middle-class environment. His upbringing as the oldest gave him the feeling of responsibility for his siblings. Over the years, he became particularly close to one of his brothers. He guided him, taught him how to play various sports, protected him from bullies at school, comforted him when he was sick, and generally took him under his wing whenever it was needed. As time passed and they all moved into adulthood, Leon noticed that he had developed the ability to get people to do what he wanted.

At first, he just took that ability as part of his grown-up personality. He heard the term "people person" and regarded himself as having that quality. He married, had children, got a good job, and began leading a decent life. He was an active and respected member of the community and a valued worker in his company. Within a few years of his marriage, he began to identify his communication capabilities as having strong manipulative power. To test it out, he tried attracting beautiful women to him. It worked.

By the time he was 30, he was not only able to manipulate and attract women to him, but he was also able to use his manipulative skills for theft and other illegal adventures. Like most manipulators, he didn't have an ounce of guilt or conscience about his activities. In fact, he reveled in what he considered successful. Yes, he was still married and was concealing all of this from his wife and family, including his brothers and sister. Through all of this, he was still especially caring and protective to the brother he loved.

Here is an example of manipulation that Leon shared. It is about a woman at work who he was sexually attracted to, not lovingly or romantically. She was in a different location in the building. He devised strategies and tactics to encounter her, have reason to be near her, and talk with her. Sometimes, the interactions were legitimate work issues. During those times, he would always sit near her or within her line of sight. Using all the usual grooming tactics, he would compliment her hair, work, contributions, and other seemingly insignificant things – generally riding the fine line between friendship and possible sexual harassment.

After a few months of this, Leon conjured a reason to actually work with her on a project. He suggested a lunch meeting. During the meeting, he was polite and professional until she said something slightly personal about her mother. That opened the door to him expressing empathy, fake of course, but a successful tactic of most manipulators. Over the next month, he continued to use his concern for her relationship with her mother to speak with her.

Eventually, Leon offered to drive his coworker home one day. During that drive, he professed a personal sense of loneliness, never admitting to having a family. He confessed some untruths about his own mother. All of this designed to bring her closer to him. Again, grooming takes time, and over a few weeks of this, she finally agreed to invite him into her home. From that point, it was not long before she was consoling him with sex.

This pattern was successful with at least six other women who he could remember. Of course, along with these "wins," he used his manipulative talents with others at work and in his social circle. Remember, manipulators are focused on winning the game, and he was good at it. It seemed that no one was aware or expressed recognition of his manipulative tactics. Reflecting on it, Leon did see signs that other people detected his activities and efforts, but no one said anything because that would bring the wrath of Leon down on them. This lifestyle went on for years.

Then, it happened. His beloved brother came down with a terrible disease and died. Leon was devastated. He went into a depression, riddled with the guilt of not saving or even bringing significant solace to his brother. He could only stand by and bear witness to his suffering and death. His manipulative mind wanted a way to gain control over his loss, but there was none. Reflecting over the years, Leon admitted that there were times when his brother wanted his assistance or advice, but he was too busy grooming one of his targets. There were times when his own wife and children requested his help or presence at a school event. Still, he was focused on devising activities and conversations to manipulate yet another target.

Several days went by. His depression grew deeper. One night he had a frightful night of dreams, visions of his brother, and memories of the funeral, the eulogy he gave, and a replay of the many deceptions and manipulative tactics with which he had hurt and controlled others for his personal pleasure. This included all the manipulation he had done with his wife, children, and other family members. It felt like a never-ending nightmare that came to a climax when his brother appeared to him.

Leon is unsure if his brother's image was part of the dream because he felt he was fully aware of his surroundings when he came to him, smiling lovingly. His brother drew himself close and gave Leon a long and strong hug, which he felt through every part of his body. Then he thanked him for caring for him all his life. Of course, Leon recalled all those times that he had manipulated his brother and family members instead. The shock of that hug and the startling feelings it created prevented him from sleeping the rest of the night.

Leon was reclusive the next day, unable to interact with anyone. His family and friends allowed him the time and space to deal with the death of his beloved brother. For Leon, it was so much more. He spent days and nights filled with guilt for all the pain and suffering he had brought to others for so many years.

As he eventually created a way to live with himself and learn how to relate with others without manipulation, Leon found a need to change his communication style and tactics. How he presented himself convinced me that he needed help. I met regularly with him over a period of a year. During that time, I came to accept his desire to reverse his manipulative ways. Also, he continued to provide many other examples of his behavior. As I listened to these admissions, I carefully scrutinized and analyzed his actions and behavior, knowing that manipulators use any and all of life's experiences to hone their ability.

After a thorough evaluation of all my interactions with him, I was ultimately able to accept his sincerity. If there is ever to be a change in manipulators, it will take some dramatic, traumatic personal experience like the death of a loved one. Time will tell if he is truly reformed. For now, we are accepting his revelations as help in understanding the mindset and behavior of manipulators.

11

Thoughts on Manipulation in Sales, Cliques, and Cults

WE CAN'T LET a book on manipulative communication tactics used against individuals conclude without commenting on the implementation of these techniques when used in groups. After all, groups are made up of individuals and a good place to practice recognizing manipulative tactics. You may not feel as vulnerable, embarrassed, humiliated, or attacked in a group setting as you do when dealing with manipulation directed at you personally. We will look at this form of manipulation in a more descriptive rather than analytical manner.

Take a moment to expand your experience as an individual target to include how manipulation is used to control groups of people. Hopefully, you will realize how controlling the *momentum of the moment* and the emotions of that moment are fundamental to cults, cliques, and even selling.

Let's start with sales. Everyone has had the experience of buying something they either didn't need, couldn't afford, or both! "*What was I thinking?*" you say, and "*How did I wind up with this?*" The reality is you may have been the target of a manipulative tactic. In sales, these tactics are usually referred to as persuasion. We defined persuasion in Chapter 1. Unlike manipulation, it always gives you the ability to walk away. Of course, sales tactics have been honed to a fine point over many years with training and practice.

We have both been in sales and trained salespeople and want to give you a different way of thinking about it. We define sales as *"helping people make good decisions."* If the product or service is right, it helps solve a problem. If it makes you happy, it is a good thing. Great salespeople make the world go 'round; they are problem solvers and people-oriented. They care about being informative and helpful. Their goal is long term relationships, and they accept not making a sale if the fit isn't right. That is never an option when you are dealing with a manipulator.

Selling becomes manipulative when a salesperson:

- withholds/hides information
- creates a false sense of urgency (act now, and you get the discount; otherwise, it's gone forever!)
- leverages your insecurities and/or uses fear
- uses any of the 24 tactics you have just learned

Salespeople are trained to be persistent. All of the techniques you have learned in Chapter 6 will help you in a sales situation. Actually, subjecting yourself to salespeople is a wonderful way to strengthen your feistiness! Remember that you can walk away ... maybe leave your wallet at home, though.

Network marketing programs are founded in manipulation. These programs are shaped and work like a pyramid, even though they have tried to repackage the concept by calling it 'network marketing.'

You can find the definition at dictionary.com:

Network Marketing - another term for pyramid selling. Network marketing is an industry that has produced millionaires but very rarely do people get rich in this business structure.

Pyramid Selling - a system of selling goods or services in which each salesperson recruits other salespeople who are expected to recruit other salespeople, resulting in a hierarchy in which each member receives compensation for the sales made by those below them.

The industry has used the tactic of "reframing" by changing the name of pyramid selling and calling it network marketing. It manipulates your view of the process from the beginning.

This structure takes advantage of the credible relationships and trust you have built over the years with your friends and family. You are told that you will get rich working from home. It usually requires you to invest in their inventory or training.

Often it's women, moms who invite you to small home gatherings and are taught to ply their friends with alcohol, cheese, and crackers and pressure them to buy or, better yet, become a rep themselves! The leaders will call you regularly to pump you up and pressure you to do more and sell more. During this process, you will see them use many of the manipulative tactics you have learned. Don't fall for it. Keep your relationships built on trust and find something you believe in to do. Otherwise, you may find friends crossing the street when they see you.

How about those cliques and cults? You may be thinking that's so high school. Not so! Robin's beloved great aunt moved to assisted living at 93 years old. When Robin called her to chat, her aunt said everyone there was in a clique, and if you sat with the "wrong" people in the cafeteria, you wouldn't be accepted by the cool crowd.

Robin also recalls her daughter starting high school, and she HAD to have a NorthFace backpack and Patagonia polar fleece jacket. When she dropped her off, she saw why. Everyone had the same thing. This is developmentally normal for junior high and high school; however, it is not healthy for a clique to control adults. There are many examples:

- The Peoples Temple (1955 - 1978)
- The Branch Davidians (1955 - 1993)
- Sullivanians (1957 – 1991)
- Children of God – Family International (1968 - Present)
- Heaven's Gate (1972 – 1997)
- Scientology

These are just a few. It can be disturbing to discover how powerful manipulative tactics are when used in a cult. We won't go into it here, but you will also find forms of manipulative tactics used in politics and religion. Stop for a moment to think about why you believe something and ask yourself how you came to hold that belief. Our primitive nature is tribal, and we are programmed to want to belong; it runs deep.

> *"Many cult groups have developed basically similar and quite compelling conversion techniques for exploiting the vulnerabilities of potential converts,"* - John G. Clark Jr., Asst. Clinical Professor of Psychiatry at the Harvard University Medical School.

Manipulation in cliques, and especially in cults, is systematic. That is, any group that you carefully scrutinize, you will find uses both manipulative tactics and a specific chronology:

- **Step 1** is to identify the target. Cults are adept at finding the vulnerable, and if you remember from our list of vulnerabilities, we are all susceptible.

- **Step 2** is the invitation to something, and it's probably something innocent and desirable. It could be a chat room, party, workshop, lunch, etc.

- **Step 3** is love-bombing ... well, you know what that is now. See tactics in Chapter 6.

- **Step 4** is seeing shiny, happy people. You want to be around them; it feels good. You may even feel that for the first time, you are really connecting with people you like.

- **Step 5** creates dependency. They will begin to give you suggestions and advice. Rules and rituals are introduced, along with rewards. You will be kept busy and away from your allies. Often there is physical deprivation, controlling your freedom.

- **Step 6** renounces loved ones who don't support your participation.

- **Step 7** introduces a new core of beliefs.

- **Step 8** is intolerance of questions and criticism, shunning of anyone who leaves, and public humiliation for the non-compliant.

We'll stop here. We intend to help you think critically, identify tactics being used, and remember you have a choice so that you will avoid being a target. As you become more adept at identifying these manipulative tactics, you will be better armed to protect yourself from manipulators. You will become better equipped to take control of the *momentum of the moment*.

12
Summary

WHAT ARE THE most important things to take from this book? Let's remember that most people have used manipulation of one sort or another to get what they want. Even an infant learns how to manipulate parents with a cry or a smile. There have already been times when you manipulated someone or some situation to achieve something you desired.

Our interpretation of manipulation in these writings has nefarious and self-serving intent. It's worth repeating the specific definition of manipulation that has prompted us to write this book. "*The use of manipulative tactics by adults on other adults for the sake of self-gain at the other's expense.*" Becoming a target of a manipulator is likely to happen to everyone, and probably multiple times during their life. As we mentioned before, life events and situations can render anyone vulnerable.

Manipulation can only occur through *communication* and the manipulator's efforts at controlling the *momentum of the moment*. Therefore the best armor you can have is the awareness, information, and preparation for the tactics they use in real-time. The self-protection techniques you have learned will enable you to shift the power and help you control the momentum of the moment.

We will all be targets at some point. However, you can maintain control and/or retake control by being aware and learning to use the techniques we have introduced. By developing proficiency in identifying manipulative communication tactics in real-time and thwarting them, you will become the most unattractive target to manipulators everywhere.

It is also worth remembering that manipulators rarely change. If change does occur, it is likely stimulated by a significant life-altering event such as the death of someone close to them or their own near-death experience. We discovered this in Leon's story. His willingness to share his story of manipulation and his brother's death gives us some hope that manipulators can change. It is best and safest to assume that they do not.

Major Takeaways From This Book:

- Manipulators are everywhere. They come in all shapes and sizes.

- Manipulators are clever and adept communicators.

- Manipulators will take advantage of everything and anything that they believe will serve their purpose.

- Manipulators always see you as a target regardless of what the relationship may be.

- You can outwit the manipulator in real-time communication!

Your Action Items:

1. Pay close attention and actively listen for manipulative tactics.

2. Remember, you ALWAYS have Free Will and, therefore, always have a choice.

3. Once you identify a manipulator, cease communication! If you can't do that, limit interaction to only superficial or essential in-person communication or writing.

4. Learn and use these techniques. Practice them out loud to become comfortable saying them.

Our sincere intention is to arm you with insight and communication techniques. This book will help you develop an actual self-protection mindset and provide you with words and behaviors to use as self-protection as the manipulation is happening. Remember, your mindset is made up of all the beliefs, attitudes, and thoughts you put into it. As an adult, you can control all of them. Take all that you are learning from this book, the information, techniques, the supporting exercises, and the App that is available to you and allow these tools to strengthen your mindset.

A strong, clear, self-constructed mindset combined with what to say and do in real-time is what will help you strengthen your ability to defend yourself. We hope that you will share this book with others who may be targets. In fact, by helping others protect themselves, you will be putting powerful thoughts, beliefs, and values into your mindset. Imagine a world where they run out of targets? We are doing our part, and now, dear reader, you have the tools to do your part to protect yourself and outwit manipulators!

NOTE-TAKING PAGE

DATE	EVENT	CONTEXT	TACTIC

DATE	EVENT	CONTEXT	TACTIC

DATE	EVENT	CONTEXT	TACTIC

Resources to Continue Learning

BOOKS

Almossawi, Ali. (2013) **Bad Arguments.** Workman Publishing.

Brown, Nina W., EdD LPC. (2008) **Children of the Self Absorbed: A guide to getting over Narcissistic Parents.** New Harbinger Publications.

Forward, Dr. Susan. (2002) **Toxic Parents.** Transworld Publishers Ltd.

Hotchkiss, Sandy. (2003) **Why is it always about you? The Seven Deadly Sins of Narcissism.** Simon and Schuster.

Lieberman, David J. (1998) **Never Be Lied to Again, 30 Covert Emotional Manipulation Tactics**. St. Martin's Griffin

Mayer, Robert. (2019) **The Art of Manipulation**. Apple Books

Peck, M. Scott. (1983) **People of the Lie: The Hope for Healing Human Evil.** Simon and Schuster.

Simon, JH. (2016) **How to Kill a Narcissist: Debunking The Myth Of Narcissism And Recovering From Narcissistic Abuse.** Simon Harrak.

Tannen, Deborah. (1986) **That's Not What I Meant.** Ballentine Book.

ARTICLES

Ackerman, Felicia (1995) *"The Concept of Manipulativeness"*, Philosophical Perspectives, 9: 335–340. doi:10.2307/2214225.

Benn, Stanley I. (1967) *"Freedom and Persuasion"*, Australasian Journal of Philosophy, 45(3): 259–275. doi:10.1080/000484067 12341211.

Brewood, Victoria. (November 2019) *"A Handy Guide to Dealing With Manipulative People"*, Thrive Global.

Long, Todd R. (2014) *"Information Manipulation and Moral Responsibility"*, in Coons & Weber 2014: 151–175. doi:10.1093/ acprof:oso/9780199338207.003.0008.

Shortsleeved, Carrie. (October 2018) *"How to Tell if Someone is Manipulating You"*, Time Magazine.

Waddell, Chloe, Van Dorn, George, March, Evita, Grieve, Rachel. (2020) *"Dominance or Deceit: The role of Dark Triad and hegemonic masculinity in emotional manipulation"*, Science Digest, Volume 166.

Zarsky, Tal Z. (2019) *"Privacy and Manipulation in the Digital Age"*, Theoretical Inquiries in Law, Volume 20.

PODCASTS

L.A. Times, Wondery. **Dirty John**.

A compelling true story of a woman who is manipulated by a man, ignoring her own intuition.

Bloomberg, Wondery. **The Shrink Next Door**.

A story about power and control and turning to the wrong person for help for decades.

Wondery. **Guru: The Dark Side of Enlightenment**.

When tragedy strikes an exclusive retreat with a self-help superstar, many people are left to wonder, how far is too far.

WEBSITES

Understanding Micro Expressions
https://www.psychologytoday.com/us/blog/
spycatcher/201112/body-language-vs-micro-expressions

Personality Disorders: Controllers, Abusers, Manipulators, and Users in Relationships
https://mental-health-matters.com/
personality-disorders-controllers-abusers-manipulators-user
s-relationships/#Histrionic_Personality

Mindset: Your Thoughts Can Release Abilities Beyond Normal Limits
https://www.scientificamerican.com/article/
your-thoughts-can-release-abilities-beyond-normal-limits/

Does Consciousness Exist Outside of the Brain?
https://www.psychologytoday.com/us/blog/think-well/201906/
does-consciousness-exist-outside-the-brain

About the Authors

ROBIN GOLINSKI Robin is the U.S. representative for the international group, Funny Women http://funnywomen.com, based in London. She is also the founder of Boston Comedy Chicks http://bostoncomedychicks.com.

Robin has a B.S. in Marketing, is a Certified Trainer with Infinite Possibilities - http://tut.com. and has continued her studies in energy, quantum physics, mediumship, and consciousness for decades.

As a member of The National Communication Association, she served as co-Chair of the Training & Development Division. She wrote the chapter on Humor and Storytelling for The Handbook of Communication Training, a first of its kind in the field of learning and development.

Her most recent work includes the co-authoring of the unique book, Outwitting the Manipulator: Protecting Yourself in Realtime. Along with Dr. Becker, they work as Executive Communication Coaches for The Speech Improvement Company.

Mindset Communication represents their interests beyond the spoken word. She's grateful to have a wonderful partner and co-author like Dr. Becker!

Dr. Dennis Becker has appeared before hundreds of clubs and organizations, from local community groups to national associations. He's been featured on radio and television programs as a guest expert and motivational speaker.

He hosted the syndicated radio series, *Talking about Talking,* and is co-host of electionspeakers.com.

Before there were podcasts, Dr. Becker created Executive Briefings and The Speakers Survival Kit, sold on tapes and CDs. Dr. Becker has taught at both Harvard and MIT, coached leaders of companies and countries, including the heads of two USA Presidential elections. He has also served as President of The New England Speech Communication Association and Chair of The Training & Development Division of The National Communication Association.

One of Dr. Becker's greatest accomplishments is, along with his wife, founding America's oldest speech coaching and communication firm, *The Speech Improvement Company,* which has served more than a million clients worldwide.

Outwitting The Manipulator: Protecting Yourself in Real-Time is Dr. Becker›s eighth book related to communication. Completing it with Robin has been inspiring and exciting for the number of people who will benefit.

We invite you to connect with us...

https://www.outwitinrealtime.com
info@outwitinrealtime.com

Group on FB: https://www.facebook.com/groups/outwit
Page on FB: https://www.facebook.com/outwitinrealtime/
Twitter: @manipulatorhelp

Download our very helpful App
from the Apple or Android App Store
OUTWIT

The free version of the app will allow you to reference techniques and keep a private journal of manipulative experiences at your fingertips.

Many will find it helpful to learn and strengthen these skills in a group or private one on one setting. They are offering the options below to help you continue developing your skills:

One on One Coaching:

Sessions can be conducted virtually. Choose either Dr. Dennis Becker or Robin Golinski to help you practice the nuances of your communication's content and delivery style when dealing with a manipulator. Focus is put on the specific challenges of your situation. If you have experienced a pattern over time, these sessions will fast track the path to breaking that pattern.

Workshops:

Public workshops are conducted both virtually and in person. These workshops focus on the content and specific manipulation tactics and self-protection techniques covered in the book as well as expanded information related to manipulation

Customized workshops are also available for individual companies, associations, and organizations. The length of these workshops can vary:

The number of participants will determine the amount of time needed to complete the workshop. Each one is highly interactive and requires that everyone take part to ensure the integration of skills. Customizing the workshop for your needs will make it even more effective. The information and activities are a profound way to change the culture of communication in any organization. Manipulative communication is not just bad for morale; it has a direct effect on productivity.

Keynote:

Dr. Dennis Becker and Robin Golinski are both experienced public speakers (see author biographies), and either can speak as keynote at your next event. It is recommended that you invite both as a dual keynote. They have a dynamic presentation style and each offers perspectives that individual listeners find compelling, informative, and even entertaining.

Youtube: Follow our Youtube channel here: http://bit.ly/OutwitManipulator

Reviews are our social proof that what we have shared in this book is making a difference.

We invite you to
Leave a Review!

Made in the USA
Middletown, DE
27 October 2022

13604804R00094